# IN THE WONDERLAND
# OF INDIAN MANAGERS

# IN THE WONDERLAND OF INDIAN MANAGERS

### SHARU RANGNEKAR

*Illustrated By*
**R K Laxman**

*Edited By*
**Pama Rangnekar**
**Kishor Aras**

## VIKAS PUBLISHING HOUSE PVT LTD

**VIKAS PUBLISHING HOUSE PVT LTD**
576, Masjid Road, Jangpura, **New Delhi**-110 014
Phones: 24314605, 24315313 • Fax: 24310879
*E-mail: helpline@vikaspublishing.com*
First Floor, N.S. Bhawan, 4th Cross, 4th Main,
Gandhi Nagar, **Bangalore**-560 009 • Phone : 2281254
F-20, Nand Dham Industrial Estate, Marol,
Andheri (East), **Mumbai**-400 059 • Phone : 28502333, 28502324
35, Palm Avenue, **Kolkata**-700 019 • Phone : 22872575
C-8, 1st floor, Nelson Chambers  15, Nelson Manickam Road,
Aminjikarai, **Chennai**-600 029 • Phone : 23744547, 23746090
Mahender Lok Apartments, Ist Floor, H No.-104,
Kankar Bagh, **Patna** - 800 020 • Phone : 2347410

*Distributors:*
**UBS PUBLISHERS' DISTRIBUTORS PVT LTD**
5, Ansari Road, **New Delhi**-110 002
Ph. 23273601, 23266646 • Fax: 23276593, 23274261
*E-mail: ubspd@ubspd.com • Internet: www.gobookshopping.com*
• 10, First Main Road, Gandhi Nagar, **Bangalore**-560 009 • Ph. 2253903
• 60, Nelson Manickam Road, Aminjikarai, **Chennal**-600 029 • Ph. 23746222
• 8/1-B, Chowringhee Lane, **Kolkata**-700 016 • Ph. 22521821, 22522910
• 5-A, Rajendra Nagar, **Patna**- 800 016 • Ph. 2672856, 2673973
• 80, Noronha Road, Cantonment, **Kanpur**-208 004 • Ph. 2305793, 2305799
• 143, M P Nagar, Zone-1, **Bhopal**-462 011 • Ph. 5203183, 5203193
• 40/7940, Convent Road, **Ernakulam**-682 035 • Ph. 2353901, 2363905

*Distributors for Western India:*
**PREFACE BOOKS**
223, Cama Industrial Estate, 2nd Floor,
Sun Mill Compound, Lower Parel (W), **Mumbai**-400 013 Ph: 24988054

Copyright © Sharu Rangnekar, 1973

| | | |
|---|---|---|
| 1st printed by Associated Personnel Services Hard Cover | : | 1973 |
| 1st reprint | : | 1974 |
| 1st paperback edition | : | 1975 |
| 25 reprints from 1975 to 1995 | | |
| 1st Vikas paperback edition | : | April 1996 |
| 1st reprint | : | June 1996 |
| 2nd reprint | : | September 1996 |
| 3rd reprint | : | February 1997 |
| 4th reprint | : | September 1997 |
| 5th reprint | : | June 1998 |
| 6th reprint | : | January 1999 |
| 7th reprint | : | March 1999 |
| 8th reprint | : | December 1999 |
| 9th reprint | : | August 2000 |
| 10th reprint | : | November 2001 |
| 11th reprint | : | May 2002 |
| 12th reprint | : | October 2002 |
| 13th reprint | : | December 2002 |
| 14th reprint | : | May 2003 |

*dedicated*
*to*
*my appreciative audience whose*
*encouragement*
*made this compilation possible*

# contents

# last word first

Most of the advice one receives is not followed. Nor does anybody expect one to do so. And yet now and then one follows a couple of wise words. This book is a result of two such wise words.

The first one was from my professor Dean Bach. He advised me, "Sharu, you talk too much. I suggest you limit your talk to what you know. This will reduce the volume considerably—and there is a chance people may listen."

While I have not followed this advice rigidly, I have kept my talks as close to my experience as possible. This has enhanced my credibility—at least I suppose so.

The second piece of advice was from my boss Ig Soisson. He was not particularly enthusiastic about my accepting lecture invitations. But when I did, he insisted that I prepare the lecture outline in advance. "If you feel it worthwhile spending some time in giving a talk," he said, "it is definitely worthwhile investing some more and putting your ideas in black and white."

Following this advice has left me with about a hundred and fifty talk outlines and most of them have found their way to articles in various periodicals in the course of time.

The person responsible for a substantial number of my talks is Prof. N.S. Ramaswamy. For some time, the two of us were known as the Laurel and Hardy of the Management World. People stopped this when they could not distinguish who was Laurel and who was Hardy as both of us grew in several dimensions.

My audiences have always been kind to me—as I usually took care to get as many friends invited to the talks as I possibly could. The response from the audiences and the readers of my articles made me think seriously about compiling the articles in a book form.

This brought up another problem. As the author, I could not decide which articles to put in and which to omit (or defer to the next book).

At his stage entered Kishor Aras—an appreciative reader who became a discriminating editor and picked up the articles for this compilation. So you now know whom to blame.

My numerous friends offered several suggestions in revising the articles and Pama did the final editing. My secretary, Homai Kerawalla did the typing. My sons and daughter contributed their bit by wondering loudly as to whether anybody would purchase my book.

SHARU RANGNEKAR

# a word again

The disappearance of the first edition in just about five months has effectively quietened down the new generation in our house which once upon a time was so ungracefully vocal in doubting whether anybody would purchase the book at all.

Our experience during the first run of the book has not been entirely unmixed. Unknown readers sent in appreciative comments and known friends wrote favourable reviews. And then there were people who prasised the cover and the printing (indicating that they have not dwelt on the book any further) and there were customers who ordered 'that Laxman's cartoon book'.

We have had some social repercussions too. At cocktail parties, we would painfully notice that a substantial section has only a brief interest in discussing the book and this often left us monopolising the company of our hosts. The sudden fall in our cocktail party invitations these days is, we hope, safely due to the spiralling inflation. To our chagrin, many visitors have been just shying away from our residence — they seem to value things other than listening to the latest reviews and the lively statistics of the number of copies sold and in balance. Such is the lack of popular interest in the higher things of life.

Nothing succeeds like success and Pama is now engrossed in editing my next book which she is titling 'Indian Intellectual in Search of a Racket'. All I can say at this stage is that it is not an authobiography. And all that my children can contribute to this venture is to suggest that I should write a book based on Laxman's cartoons rather than the other way round.

Kishor Aras and his enthusiastic band Dixit, Churi and Hirachand (May their tribe prosper!) have spared no efforts to push the book and it is to their credit that the first print has been pushed out so soon. All strength to them — to push out the second print too.

SHARU RANGNEKAR

xii

# a paperback word

I have been showered with criticism from many quarters, both from within the press and outside, regarding some abstract deficiencies in my book. As one interested in environmental peace and harmony, I have shunned these unkind souls and have been fairly successful in avoiding a major conflict by keeping myself in blissful isolation.

But one material criticism vehemently expressed and which I dare not disregard is concerning the price, though it is no consolation that the criticism came from those who borrowed the book. As one habitual borrower reported, with low-priced books the follow-up by the lender for the return of the book is very lukewarm and one can easily build a good collection. His grouse was that owing to the high price of the book he was under constant pressure to return it and eventually my book could not adorn the shelves of his library.

Since the number of book-borrowers is a large multiple of the number of purchasers, an inexpensive edition became essential to appease the borrowers in particular and to serve mankind in general. Another strong motivation was my keen desire to make some modest contribution towards arresting the inflationary trends in this country. I am sure that this paperback edition will lead to a wider circulation of the book.

SHARU RANGNEKAR

# after a generation

Two hard-cover editions and over thirty paperback editions is perhaps a record in Indian management literature. To me the real surprise is to meet so many people who remember the book 'In the Wonderland of Indian Manager'. Some have actually read it.

Lately, I have been meeting managers who tell me that their fathers gave them the book to read — and I suddenly realise that almost a generation has passed since the book was first printed at the beginning of 1973.

There have been great changes in this generation — even in the management field. Designations have changed — there are more Presidents than M.Ds these days. Inflation has spread from prices to management designation — and recently to management salaries. Computers — a mystery a generation ago — are common and understood by all except a few at the top management levels.

So I face a question: Is this book valid even after such a catastrophic generation? Does it need to be updated?

I went through the book again only to find that my description of management foibles seems to be as relevant today as it was a generation ago. Decisions are still being avoided actively, Jagirdari system is prepotent, interviewers are playing their games with candidates, the Feudal Vizirs and the Cocktails Managers are confusing the babes in the woods and illiterate managers abound.

In short, the more management changes in India — the more it remains the same!

So I do hope that this improved edition — improved in size, get-up (and price) will serve another generation of managers.

SHARU RANGNEKAR

# acknowledgements

Acknowledgement is due to the following periodicals which published one or several articles included in this book:

1. Aeromag, My 72
2. ATMA, Ap/Jn 67, Oc/De 68, Ja/Ma 72
3. Banking, Se 70
4. Bombay Civic Journal Ap 68, Se 68, Jl 69, Jn 70
5. Bombay Market, Ma 72
6. Bombay Productivity Council N/L, Oc/No 67
7. Business Herald, Jn 71, Jl 72
8. Calcutta Productivity Council:Newsletter Annual:1966, 1968
9. Chartered Secretary, Ja 72, My 72
10. CIS India Newsletter, Se/Oc 71, No/De 71
11. Columbia Journal of World Business, Ma/Ap 69, Ja/Fe 70
12. DLW Bulletin, Fe 69, Ma 69, My 69, Jn 69, Se 69, Ma 70, Jl 70, Au 72
13. Durgapur Steel Tidings, My 69
14. Electrical & Mechanical Engg., Ap 70
15. ETA Bulletin, My 72
16. FACT Engineer, Oc 69
17. FFP Technical Journal (HEC Ranchi), Jn 68
18. Fortschirittlichen Betriebsfuhrung (German), De 66
19. Gospel, Oc/De 70
20. Hexagon, Jn 66
21. HTS Digest, Oc 69, Jl 71, Ap 72
22. ICSI Souvenir, De 71
23. IE (1) Golden Jubilee Number, Ma 70
24. Indian Buyer, Jl 68, Oc 68
25. Indian Liberatarian, Ma 72
26. Indian Journal of Marketing, No 71
27. Indian Management, Jl/Au 68, Au 69

# how to avoid
# making decisions

WHEN missionaries started preaching Christianity in Africa, they caused some confusion with their colour scheme of a 'white' Jesus and a 'black' devil. There was a real spurt in conversions when some genius changed the colour scheme declaring Jesus 'black' and devil 'white'

A similar confusion has taken place in the field of management in India. Foreign professors or Indians imported straight from foreign universities without contamination with Indian industry are spreading the gospel: 'management is decision-making". This caused untold hardships to the young graduates of the management institutes when they entered Indian industry and attempted decision-making.

So the time has come to reveal the Truth: "in India management is decision-avoiding". Some sceptics wonder whether the confusion caused by the two-year-full-time or three-yer-part-time instruction in management institutes can be cleared with a single stroke. We should not worry about these sceptics because we know: "Truth shall prevail".

In India, it is as important to learn ways of avoiding decisions as it is to learn ways of decision-making in America. The first decision-rule of Indian Management is: If you can avoid it, don't take it.

## DECISION AVOIDING VS. DECISION DELAYING

Laymen often confuse decision delaying with decision avoiding. Delaying is rather a passive and negative

3

activity. It does not have the positive and active impact of decision avoiding. An effective manager will not be sitting back simply delaying decisions. He will be on his feet where decisions are asked for and will avoid them. He will keep initiative in his hands and will not allow 'decision-by-default'

Thus, even if the ultimate result is the same, the approach is very much different. Most of the methods available for avoiding decisions are equally effective in delaying decisions. But an efficient manager will stand out by his approach. He will not delay the decision—thus increasing his workload for tomorrow since the problem is likely to be brought up again. He will avoid the decision once and for all. The second decision-rule, therefore, is: If you can avoid it, don't delay it.

Even where it is impossible to avoid decision and the only alternative is to delay it, the active manager is clearly distinguished from the passive one The passive manager will delay by being too busy, going on leave, putting the problem at the bottom of the pending pile, going on tour and if all these fail falling sick. The active, decision-avoiding manager will counsel a deliberate delay, e.g.:

"**Re: Cycle Stand for Workers**: The industrial situation in India is in a melting pot. It is essential to allow time to stabilise the situtation', the 'macro-situation' has to be clarified. so I suggest that this cycle-stand proposal be delayed idefinitely..."

## PASS-THE-BUCK APPROACH

The first step to decision-avoiding is to determine whether we should avoid the decision by ourselves or "pass the buck". The third decision-rule states: **If you can get somebody else to avoid the decision, don't avoid it yourself**.

*****Committee Method**: The most popular method of passing the buck is to appoint a committee to 'review the problem'

4

This method has been patronised very widely by government authorities but it is by no means their monopoly Non-government sectors also have found this method extremely useful for decision-avoiding Although in many cases, the very act of appointing committees will effectively ensure decision-avoiding, a wise manager will doubly ensure the result by taking the following meaures:

1. **Make the committee as large as possible:**

   A committee of three may suddenly get to a decision. The possibility is greatly alleviated if the membership is increased to nine. Research has revealed the mathematical rule (known as the fourth decision-rule)): **The possibility of avoiding decision increases in proportion to the square of the number of members in the committee.** Committees with membership of thirty and above rarely reach any significant decision (e.g. National Integration Council).

2. **Make the committee meeting difficult:**

   This can be done by appointing a sick chairman, members geographically as distant as possible, etc. In recent times, geographical distance has been a very effective deterrent to committee meetings. The airlines are helping actively through staggered strikes by pilots, air-hostesses, mechanics, etc. In the case of railways, any agitation on food, politics or language is adequate. For example the agitations to "Remove English" in the north and to "Remove Hindi" in the south were immediately effective in removing trains everywhere!

3. **Make the committee incompatible:**

   At least two members of the committee should have a previous record of proved hostility or at least a dominating attitude. Others will develop hostility as the committee work proceeds.

**\*Abominable No-man Method:** Many companies have an invaluable asset which rarely figures on their balance-sheet. It is the "Abominable no-man". The basic characteristic of this person is his infinite capacity to say "no". Consequently, even a threat to refer the matter to A.N. compels the initiator to drop his proposal.

*Bottomless Joe Method: In the absence of the availability of A.N., some companies resort to the "Bottomoless Joe". B.J. has the exceptional quality that any matter referred to him is guaranteed to get lost. He is invaluable to his employers because he cannot or will not complete any job assigned to him and is thus very convenient for avoiding decisions.

Needless to say, A.N. and B.J. are extremely useful as members of any committee appointed to avoid decisions.

*Make it a Policy Matter: In circumstances where committees cannot be appointed and A.N. or B.J. are not readily available, the buck can still be passed to the higher management by making the problem a policy matter, e.g.

"There has been a proposal for a cycle-stand for workers. This basically forms a part of our employee-benefit scheme and consequently cannot be considered in isolation. In due course, the top management should consider this proposal while reviewing our wage-structure, benefit scheme, etc...."

In criminal cases, "insanity" is the ultimate plea. Similarly, in management action or inaction, "policy" is the ultimate convenient label.

*Suggest a Survey: Looking at the practices of others is a sure way of creating confusion and delay, e.g.:

"I suggest a survey be carried out in our geographical area as well as in our industry to find out location and industry practices vis-a-vis provision of vehicular parking (e.g. cycle-stand) for employees reporting on duty..."

*Appoint a Consultant: This is rather a desperate move and should be resorted to when other remedies are not available. If a proper consultant is chosen and his terms are made ambiguous enough his report will create enough confusion and hostility so that the original problem will be lost.

## DO-IT-YOURSELF DECISION-AVOIDING

Situations arise where a manager is unable to pass the buck and is compelled to avoid decisions by himself. In such cases, the manager may use any of the following approaches:

**Scare the Initiator**: The methods available for this purpose are:

*****Tantrum Method**: This is a somewhat ancient method, but is still efective. When the initator comes with his proposal, you should throw a tantrum, e.g.: "Cycle-stand for workers! Oh, what a proposal and what a time to bring it up! The bearing on the starting machine has broken down, the compound wall has cracked due to the last earthquake and my ulcers are bothering me again! Can you not think of anything more significant than a cycle-stand?

*****Hush-hush Method**: Alternately, you may warn the initiator that he is rushing in where "angels fear to tread", e.g

"Cycle-stand for workers! Sh-sh-sh, talk low. This matter is already with the top brass and there are wheels-within-wheels. If I were you, I would just keep quiet and tell anybody who talks about this problem to keep his trap shut..."

*****More-details-please Method:** If you keep on asking for more and more details, the initiator will give up his proposal sooner or later e.g

"Regarding your proposal (cycle-stand for workers) we regret to note that full details have not been made available. Before the proposal can be considered further, we would like to have the following details in quintuplicate:

1. Dimensions of standard cycles with expected variation.
2. Average laden and unladen weight with usual variations.
3. Estimated capacity requirements by quarters in the next seven years.
4. Possible modes of construction with estimated cost (Please enclose 3 competitive quotations each)
5. All other relevant or significant details available at your end..."

**\*Double-talk Method**: If you have mastered the jargon of management, you can confuse the initiator, e g

"You are talking about cycle-stand for workers. Do you realise that is just a method of their expressing the lack of mutual trust. So we must look upon the problem as a symptom and not as a disease. What must we do to create an atmosphere of mutual trust or harmony? Not granting material benefits, but intereacting with the workers to create a feeling ,of unity..."

**\*No-problem-exists Method**: Deny the very existence of the problem, e.g.:

"What is this about a cycle-stand? We have been running this factory for 15 years without a cycle-stand. Everybody knows that cycles can stand without a cycle-stand. Why do you want a cycle-stand? Why do you want to bring up an imaginary problem?...

**\*That's-your-problem Method**: Throw it back at the initiator, e.g.:

"I am sure you would like to work according to our responsibilities and authorities. The matter of a cycle stand is something within your responsibility and authority and I suggest you deal with the problem considering all the allied and relevant aspects..."

8

# the jagirdari system
# in indian industry

WE have been talking about productivity for years.

We even observed a 'Productivity Year' which started a phenomenal decline in our industrial production. In most of our talking was stressed 'techniques'—creating an impression that we can increase productivity merely by applying work measurement or linear programming or budgetary control.

It is probably high time that we faced some facts. The root cause of our deficiency does not lie in the lack of techniques or the lack of resources. It lies in our approach in our mind. the preamble of UNESCO states: "War starts not on the battlefield, but in the minds of men. And it is in the minds of men that bastions of peace must be erected..." Similarly, we have to lay the foundation of our industrial growth in our own minds.

## IN THE BAD OLD DAYS

In the days prior to industrialisation, the ambition of a dashing youg man in India was to acquire a 'Jagir'. A scholar, a poet, a man of wits or a man of sword dreamt of demonstrating his talents to a prince and getting a jagir as a recognition or a reward. Then he could sit back and relax. The jagir would not only maintain him during his lifetime, but would also pass on to his progeny. To acquire a jagir by one's own talent or by heredity was a matter of 'kismet'. Once one had a jagir, one had one's living assured.

Theoretically, every jagirdar was supposed to fulfil certain obligations to the overlord. But in practice, the obligations were invariably neglected. If the overlord really desired some assistance from his jagirdars, he would have to offer something special as compensation.

This was characteristic of the feudal system. The feudal parasites were supposed to pass out with the feudal system, once industrialisation took its hold.

But we Indians have a unique sense of synthesis. Instead of replacing the fendal system with the industrial system, we have synthesised the two and created a jagirdari system within our industry.

## THE JAGIRDARI APPROACH

The jagirdari approach to industry started with the family management. The Indian managing agencies introduced hereditary feudal management in industry An industrial unit was administered like a jagir with members of the family manning the key positions. Changes in the managerial hierarchy often depended on the family pulls and feuds and often industrial expansion was undertaken to provide for family expansion.

As a result, the industrial units are run not for their longterm prosperity, but for the short-term benefits of the family. The incentive to productivity in such an atmosphere is rather limited. A glaring example in this regard is the plight of our cotton textile industry. During the Second World War, the textile mills made windfall profits and squandered them on high dividends. When the time came to modernise their machinery, the valuts were empty.

When the government started industrial enterprise, new jagirdars from the civil service entered the industrial field. The managerial jobs were valued in terms of the corresponding civil service grades. While jobs in the family-managed concerns had an uncertain tenure (except for family members), the jobs in the public sector had a steel-strong tenure. The result was the separation of 'work' from 'job' A person got his emoluments and perquisites because of his job—whether he worked effectively or not. This reduced work to almost a hobby—with a disastrous effect on productivity.

## DEMOCRATISATION OF JAGIRDARI

We live in a democratic set-up. So we synthesised the democratic approach with the feudal system and the industry to come up with a 'jagirdari for all" slogan. The clerical staff and the labour got unionised and the unions kept up the pressure for more emoluments and facilities—without reference to productivity. In fact, productivity was discouraged to facilitate greater employment. While you could get a graduate to work as a clerk 8 hours a day in the town for Rs 150 a month, if you put him on your payroll he would refuse to do even half the work at twice the salary. A similar situation exists regarding labour. It is getting increasingly difficult to get any output in spite of increasing emoluments.

So in India today we find Parettos Law operating in a strange field. The law explains a peculiar characteristic of inventories as: "20 per cent of the items account for 80 per cent of the value". The law is now applicable in many areas of clerical work with the format: "20 per cent of the staff accounts for 80 per cent of the work."

Periodically, the government declares its intention to cut staff by 10 per cent. (It is an arithmetical miracle as to how the staff doubles itself every five years in spite of a 10 per cent cut every year!) A department head once told me that he can cut his staff by 25 per cent if he is allowed to weed out the scum that produces nothing.

Everybody-for-his-rights-and-nobody-for-his-obligations approach is fast spreading. Just the other day, a pintsize person approached a labour officer for a manual job. "Look at the big strong man in the gang you want to work with,"

13

said the labour officer, "would you be able to work as much as they can?" "I may not be able to work as much as they can," repiled the small man, "but I can surely work as much as they will."

A foreign consultant told another story the other day When he came across a clerk doing no work, he asked him. "Why don't you work?"

"Why should I?" asked the clerk.

"So that you can get promoted and make more money" replied the consultant.

"What is the point?" asked the clerk.

"So that you can retire early if you want to and won't have to work," replied the consultant.

"I am not working now," pointed out the clerk.

The consultant also expressed his surprise at the clamour for 'private offices' in India. When he asked why we require so many private offices, he was told that privacy is essential for work. "In India, every imaginable activity is carried out in public," exclaimed the consultant, "except work for which privacy is essential!"

## EFFECT OF JAGIRDARI

This would all have been funny and fine—if we could afford it. Unfortunately, the parasites created in the jagirdari system are throttling our economy. A few princes with their privy purses was a small luxury. But millions of workers, clerks, supervisors and managers want to have privy purses without adequate contribution and this will surely ruin us.

The spirit is spreading fast and animating even the next generation i.e. students. The passion for getting something for nothing is revealed in the demonstrations for getting degrees without learning.

14

Many-a-time people indulge in the quest for parasitic living because it is within their constitutional rights. The crux of the matter, however, is somewhat different. There is a story of a person who visited a barber shop and requested the barber to shave him without the usual soliloquy. But the barbar could not resist the temptation to address a captive audience. When the customer complained to the shop-owner, the owner pointed out that the Constitution of India allows free speech. "The Constitution of India can stand his talk," claimed the customer, "but my constitution cannot."

Thus, what is feasible under our political constitution may not be practical under our economic situation. As such, efforts are essential at all levels to abolish jagirdari in our industry and to ensure productivity. We can no longer consider this somebody else's problem. There is a sotry of a man who started drilling a hole in the bottom of the boat while it was in midstream. The other occupants shouted, "What are you doing?" "Mind your own business", replied the man. "I am boring a hole under my seat, and not under yours." It is high time we realise that all of us are in the same boat and the economic leaks will ruin us all. As John Donne wrote·

No man is an island in himelf, he is part of the mainland.

If a clod be washed away, Europe is less.

Any man's death diminishes me

Never send to know for whom the bell tolls:

It tolls for thee.

15

# strange ritual
# called recruitment

A ritual may be defined as a practice which has no logical relationship to the objective-but only a symbolic subjective link. We, the sophisticated executives, feel that rituals are the monopoly of the ignorant masses. We feel there is no place for rituals in the scientific and systematic management of today. Consequently, one is taken by surprise when one suddenly comes across an evidence of rituals in modern management. Just the other day, it was revealed that one of our foremost progressive concerns consults astrologers before signing important contracts.

This is a clear-cut open ritual. However, if one looks carefully, into many of our management practices, one finds rituals hidden under a thin veneer of apparent sophistication. We shall presently look into the ways in which we handle recruitment and how we have managed to convert it into a ritual.

## RECRUITMENT IN MODERN MANAGEMENT

In a recent study in U.S.A., it was found that most companies would not think of stinting on efforts to ensure that they get the capital equipment most suitable to their requirement. But these same companies are only too likely to skimp on the job of providing the people who will be needed to operate the machinery or to manage the operators. This lopsided method of managing usually stems from the company's failure to understand that planning for personnel is as important as planning for equipment or for operation. The American Management

Association has estimated that the average company devotes 98 per cent of its planning efforts to sales, engineering, production, capital investment and budgetary functions and only 2 per cent to planning for personnel. This obviously overlooks the fact that engineering designs, production facilities, maketing arrangements and operating cash cannot be fully effective if the right amount or right talent is not available at the right time.

The situation is not very much different in India. The ·shortage of qualified personnel is evident from the size of recruitment advertisements—a size which a few years ago used to be identified only with the gala premiere of epoch-making films. Yet our procedure of recruitment is not substantially different from the days when a company used to purchase a 'NO VACANCY' sign together with its nameboard.

## THE RITUAL OF RECRUITMENT

**The High Priests:** First, let us look at the personnel manning the recruitment sections. In many companies, the Personnel Department competes with the Filing and Mail Departments for discards from the rest of the organisation. These discards or surplus bodies are likely to gravitate to man the recruitment section and become the high priests of the Recruitment Ritual.

**Announcement:** The first step in the Recruitment Ritual is the "Situations Vacant" advertisement. Normally, one would expect the advertisment to be drafted to attract candidates. However, just as social clubs are meant not to get people in, but to keep them out, the advertisements are meant not to attract candidates but to repel as many of them as possible. Here are a few samples repellents in popular use.

(a) Asking for qualification and experience irrelevant or out of proportion to the job: We can see advertisements which ask for chartered accountants or person with 8 years' experience in clerical vacancies. One wonders that clerical job requires that much experience! In a recent case, the addvertisement specified five years' experience in computer programming for a programmer's job. They may have as well written to the few persons in India having such experience instead of spending on the advertisement.

(b) Insisting on release from present employers: This approach is generally followed by the public sector companies which seem to bend backwards to discourage any good candidates.

(c) Warning that only those ready to put in hard work need apply: This is at best a waste of advertisement space since applicants admitting unwillingness to work hard are not known to exist at least before taking up a job.

**Application Form:** Forms represent the ultimate creative activity in our times. In designing application forms, many organisations excel themselves. The time when you could give your qualifications and experience on one side of a quarto sheet and call it a day is gone. In modern application forms—which aim to uncover a wealth of information in at least four closely printed quarto size pages—you do not get to these aspects till the third page. Details such as your height and weight, your grandfather's age and occupation, etc. precede.

**Interview:** The foregone are merely the preliminaries. The ritual really comes into its own at the interview stage. Most companies take one of the following two approaches (although cases are known where both approaches are followed simultaneously):

(i) **Hurdle Race Approach:** In this case, the candidates are processed one by one through various interviewing personnel most of whom ask identical questions, e.g. "Why do you want to change your job?" "Why are you not married?," etc.

21

(ii) **Inquisition Approach:** In this case, a candidate is surrounded by half-a-dozen interviewers who shoot at him—and some of them occasionally shoot at each other for a change.

**Test:** This is a recent sophistication. In the good old days, you could reject a candidate because he came from the wrong community or had a squint or reminded you of your mother-in-law. Now-a-days, you give him a test either before or after the interview and still reject him essentially on the same grounds. There are tests designed by qualified people to test specific attributes. However, many organisations devise their own tests which require knowledge of such important items as: "Who was the father of Cleopatra?" or "What is the population of Finland?" There is a story about the way tests are used. Once an executive hired a psychologist to assist in the selection of his secretary. To the three final candidates the psychologist asked separately the same question: "What is 1 and 1?" "Two" said the first girl. "Eleven" said the second girl. "It can be two or it can be eleven," said the third girl. "Now we have three types of thought processes," the psychologist summed up, "one is the obvious type, one is the devious type and the third is the comprehensive type. Which one do you prefer?"

The executive replied, "Give me the blonde with long legs."

**THE INTERVIEWERS**

Interviewers play a major role in the Recruitment Ritual. The sole objective of interview is to find reasons for rejecting the candidate. This is best done by trapping the candidate—a few sample methods are illustrated below:

(i)  Interviewer: "Have you read the Company Law."
     Candidate:   "Yes."
     Interviewer: "What does Section 303 relate to? or "Under what sections can company Directors be sent to jail upto 3 months?"

```
Candidate:    ! !
Remarks:      Reject.
```

(ii)
```
Interviewer:  "What is your hobby?"
Candidate:    "Table-tennis."
Interviewer:  "Who was the Table-tennis World
              Champion in 1956?"
Candidate:    ! !
Remarks:      Reject.
```

(iii)
```
Interviewer:  "You are interested in Production or
              Sales?"
Candidate:    (Remembering that the post advertised
              mentioned sales):
              "Sales"
Interviewer:  "Field Sales or Sales Development?"
Candidate:    (Tries hard to remember the advertise
              ment—which had nothing mentioned about
              these aspects; ultimately blurts out): "Sales
              Development
Remarks:      Not interested in Field Sales, hence
              rejected.
```

## THE APPLICANTS

The most important participants of the Recruitment Ritual are the applicants. Let us meet some of the more interesting types:

(i) **Post-card Applicant:** Whatever may be the post, whether it be that of a Despatch Clerk or a Chief Accountant, there is at least one person who does not consider it worth any higher investment than 10 paise. The post-card applicant shows a great expertise on space utilisation. Unfortunately none has passed through the rigours of interviews, otherwise companies cramped for office space could well use such a person.

(ii) **The Complete Applicant:** This represents the other extreme from the post-card applicant. He believes in giving full details and sends about 4 to 6 oz, of closely typed material. It includes his mark sheets from early school days upto the end of his examination career and a wad of testimonials earned thereafter. A systematic person in this class often gives reference in his covering letter such as "see enclosure xiv and enclosure xxxii for further details "

(iii) **All-round Applicant:** This person has such an all-round experience that he is qualified for any post whatsoever. Instances are known where at a tender age as low as 21, the applicant had acquired an all-round experience in purchasing, sales, production, store-keeping, accounts, costing, audit, personnel and typing.

(iv) **Professional Applicant:** Often an almost illegible 7th carbon copy of the details of the candidate is received as application. This is from the professional applicant. According to informed sources,his procedure is as follows: He gets up in the morning, looks into the situations vacant columns and notes down all posts above a certain salary range. Then he types out a common letter giving details and addresses it to all the advertisers with no discrimination as to qualifications or experience asked for. A further sophistication in this class in the one who has cyclostyled details as well as the application letter. Instances are known where a professional applicant has gone so far as to get the whole darned thing printed.

(v) **The Connected Applicant:** In contrast to the above mentioned applicants, this applicant deals very briefly with such minor details as qualifications and experience and goes on to write an essay on the important aspect as to how well he is "connected" He give the details of all his relatives on father's side, mother's side and wife's side. The advantage that the connected applicant offers to the employer is obviously the status—since the employer would be known in high circles as having employed such a well-connected personality

(vi) **Evergreen Applicant:** Whatever may be the age-limit set in the advertisement, you will always hear from a few applicants who have had 40 years' experience. These persons are generally over 60, but to state in their own words "have energy and enthusiasm and working capacity twice (or many more times) that shown by the present generation."

(viii) **Bargain Application:** These applicants after bargains to the employer such as: "You can get 3 brothers at the price of 2", or "If you employ me, my wife will work as my secretary-without emoluments " Since these offers create problems in the usual interview procedure, these applicants generally do not progress any further.

(viii) **The One-in-a-Hurry:** This applicant is so much concerned about the promptnes of providing services and saving money for his prospective employer that he wants to eliminate all interviews that cost money and time and calls on the employers personally on the day the advertisment appears.

## SELECTION

In spite of all-out efforts to reject everybody, a time comes when one is forced to sit down and select somebody. This is indeed hard on the person concerned. Like a passenger already in the train when it enters a station, he has tried his best to keep out everybody he can—but ultimately he has to admit somebody in.

The selection is easier when one of the candidates is related to somebody in the top management. When such is not the case, tossing a coin or rolling a dice could give a selection—which may not be much different from the actual one, since the exact requirements of the job and the relevant attributes of the candidates are rarely available at this juncture. Any female candidate is automatically rejected for management cadres in private sector since, we seem to be fully convinced that we can have a female

Prime Minister but not a female departmental head in our office.

The selection marks the end of the Recruitment Ritual— and sometimes the beginning of the next one: the Training Ritual.

**FOUR**

## the tragedy
## that is training

NOT too long ago, a manager—when found lacking in any aspect—was expected to work harder and become better. In those days, hard work—like castor oil—was the cure of many ills.

The days have changed: today, as soon as a manager is found lacking in any aspect, he is earmarked for training. Even those who are not particularly deficient in any specific aspect, are expected to become better by training. Just as nudists believe that more sunlight on a greater part of the body means better health, organisations seem to believe the more training to more managers means better management.

So the time has come to study how this training is planned and how it is organised.


## COMMON APPROACHES TO TRAINING

The study of the organisational planning for training has revealed the following five approaches.

1. **Minced-meat Approach:** This approach is characteristic of production-oriented organisations. You put the raw material at one end and you get the finished produce at the other end. You put meat at the top the grinder and receive minced-meat at the bottom. Similarly, you send your manager-designate for management development course and—lo and behold!— here comes back the developed manager! But this does not happen and the organisations are disgusted by the

fact the chaps who return after a three months residential management development course, are nowhere near to the finished product.

2. **Spare-parts Approach:** Some organisations are more modest in their expectations. They do not expect a finished product from the raw material. They only expect the particular wrong characteristic to be replaced by the right one—something like sending the car to get the faulty carburetter replaced. They expect that the manager who does not delegate adequately will start delegating when he goes through a three-day seminar on delegation. In spite of the modest expectations, these organisations also seem to be frustrated about the results.

1. **Assembly-line Approach:** Some organisations are more realistic. They realise that in some cases a single operation may not give the result. As assembly-line of operations is essential to finish the product. So they arrange a series of courses to 'finish' the managerial staff. However, success seems to elude even in this approach.

2. **Fringe-benefit Approach:** Some organisation seems to view training in a different light altogether. They do not seem to be worried about the development aspect. They emphasise the ex-gratia leave, expense paid residence in a location with good climate, etc and include it in their fringe-benefits scheme—somewhere between a holiday bunglow and supernnuation benefit. The various training courses are then graded in order of their attractiveness and are available to the staff according to their level of seniority—similar to the allocation of the Puri bungalow during Puja holidays.

3. **Nobless-oblige Approach:** Here the training is held as an unavoidable evil. A company with a good name has got to send persons for training courses—as patronage. The person sent is the one who can be most conveniently spared. One company ultimately appointed a Training Officer, when they found it difficult to spare persons for

training from its regular staff on all occasions. The job of this Training Officer now is to attend traing courses.

## STATUS SYMBOL

The greatest development in the development in the field of training is the phenomenon called the 'Management Trainee'. This is a blue-eyed-boy who is expected to wander around the company watching people working and thus learning how to do things—so that later on he can supervise the work as a manager. It is generally considered impractical to create engineers by asking the aspirants to look at an engine. However, the idea of creating managers by asking the trainees to look at people being managed, is gaining in popularity.

In fact, it is now a status-symbol to have management trainees—or at least advertise for some. The other day, I met the Personnel Manager of a company which had just put out a large advertisement for management trainees. "Going for a big expansion?" I asked him. "No", he replied, "we do not really plan to add to our payroll. But the boss wants our show to keep up with the Joneses."

Even those who actually recruit management trainees seem to spend most of their efforts on drafting attractive advertisements. Training schemes are rarely worked out and trainees are left on their own. "This is an interesting experience," remarked a trainee, "we are getting a pension at the beginning of our career rather than waiting till the end."

## TRIBES OF PREACHERS

Now let us look at the organisation of training courses. With an increasing demand for training, it only needs a supply to start the orgy of training. The supply is provided by various bodies like management training institutes, professional associations, management consultants and

31

commercial quacks. The faculty, however, comes from four major sources:

1. **Professors:** These are the lean, hungry-looking bush-shirt-clad individuals who can spout more jargon in an hour about management than a manager is likely to encounter in his whole natural life. They emphasise the essential technqiues of profit optimisation—while in real life, managements seem to be making good money without following any of them. For long courses a few from this tribe are essential—on account of their stamina.

2. **Executives:** While the participants are awed by the jargon from the academic tribe, they are more impressed by the plump, prosperous-looking, well-dressed fellow executive. Consequently, there is an increasing demand for executive preachers. This has led to wonders. Executives have been rummaging through books that their secretaries have hastily collected from assorted sources and dictating copious notes on such unheard of things as management by participation, channels of communication, etc. The gap between preaching and practice goes on widening as the executive preachers improve in their preaching.

3. **Consultants**: The resources necessary for starting management consultancy in India are very modest: a board and a pot of paint: No profession requires fewer qualifications and experience than that of management consultancy in India. This tribe provides a sizable supply of faculty for training courses—

4. **Tourists:** Everybody is an expert 500 miles from his home-town. If he crosses the seas, he becomes a foreign expert, which is an improvement comparable to that from a cock to a peacock. If he can speak English, he is ipso facto a very desirable faculty for any training course. If he is British, he is good for attracting a sizeable number of participants. If he is American (that being the limit of all foreign expertise), the

32

sponsors of the training course can pick and choose from the aspiring participants. Europeans, Canadians and Australians fall somewhere in between these two limits. Asians, Latin Americans and Africans do not rate very high as foreign experts for the purpose of the training faculty—unless they have British or American qualifications.

## TRICKS OF THE TRADE

With the increase in the number of organisations conducting continual training courses, a certain degree of competition has crept in the field. This has led to a clever device to attract participants. Some typical devices are as follows:

1. **Special Rates**: Most organisations offer concessional rates to their members. Since the members get very little else for their membership, they are induced to take advantage of the concession. This is similar to the 'Grand Reduction Sale' practised almost continuously by many retail stores.

2. **Package Rates:** Offering package courses for 2 or more persons at an advantageous rate has proved attractive in certain cases. Similar to the package offer of toothbrush—tooth paste—shaving cream, there is a package offer to train materials manager—purchase assistant—stores clerk in a 3-level materials management course—at a package rate.

3. **Package Deals:** This takes advantage of the ethusiasm of the executive preachers to be on the faculty. In one course at a hill station, the deal offered to the executives of the company was:

A.   For sending 1 participant:
One faculty member will be invited for 1 lecture (1 day stay).

B.   For sending 2 participants:
One course director will be invited to stay for one week.

C. For sending 2 participants:
One course director will be invited together with his family to stay for the entire duration of the course.

4. **Reciprocal Deals:** In this deal, the executive of Company A sends a participant to the course organised by the Institute X in return for a participant to be sent from Comapny B to the course organised by the Institute Y-Obviously, the executive from Company A is the Chairman of the Institute Y, while the executive from Company B is the Secretary of the Institute X.

The situation could not have been more comical—but for two facts. First, it represents a waste of our scarce resources. Secondly, it minimises the effective training actually imparted—and, all said and done, the paucity of our managerial talents, as well as our inefficient management practices, emphasise the urgency of effective training.

# how to promote without
# really promoting

WE are in the midst of an era in which this land seems to be full of rather peculiar people. We have students who won't study and teachers who won't teach. Our law and order men create disorder. Our operators refuse to operate. Our salesmen won't sell. Our servicemen won't give service.

And a part of this overall mess are our workers who won't work and our managers who won't manage.

This mess was not created overnight nor was it the work of any single group of people. It took mighty teamwork and a long period of time. Everybody did his bit. Our politicians helped by instilling a strong sense of rights and privileges obviating the sense of duty and the productivity required to carry this burden. Our officials in the Government helped by creating an ever-expanding bureaucracy without reference to the scant resources of the nation that have to bear the burden. Our businessmen helped by playing a game with the tax authorities leading to a spiral of tax imposition and tax evasion.

And our managers did their bit by neglecting the most important resource of an enterprise: Personnel.

## PREACHING AND PRACTICING

In real life, one has to be tolerant of some gap between preaching and practicing. However, in India, our degree of tolerance is so high that it can be summed up only as "simpleton living and high preaching." We do not seem to be bothered by the tie up of stone-age practices with atomic-age preachings.

This is most evident in our personnel policies. Most managers proudly declare that their personnel is their most valuable resource.

They acknowledge the fact that the material and capital resources can produce as big a loss as they can produce a profit—if the personnel handling the material and capital resources is inadequate.

And yet, when a project is planned, personnel is the last thing anybody worries about. It is not unusual to get the machinery installed and declared ready for operation and then start looking for the personnel required—from the operator to manager! Again, companies spend appreciable resources to plan sales, production, maintenance and capital investments. But planning efforts on personnel, if at all expended, are likely to be scanty.

## SEARCHING IN THE DARK

Why does this happen? Even where management seems to be aware of the importance of planning and developing personnel, there seems to be always some trouble to get the right man at the right time.

The main reason seems to be that our knowledge about the 'right' qualities required for a job is awfully meagre. It is relatively easier to determine the 'right' material or the 'right machine for a job as the qualities can be objectively evaluated. One can talk about a material having the right tensile strength or a machine giving the correct tolerances. But how to we decide what is the essential quality for a job? Why does Raman sell better than Krishnan? Why does Basu get a higher production than Borkar? Why is Patel a better administrator than Rao? Ask these questions to five different people who know both the performers and you are likely to get six different answers.

So what do we do? We presume some obvious external characteristics like qualifications and experience to be vital. Ram has 10 years experience while Krishnan has only 8. So we decide that 10 years selling experience is essential for the Sales Manager's position. The fact that Sundaram with 15 years experience is doing worse than Krishnan or that Krishnan is unlikely to give a better performance even after 2 years is conveniently forgotten.

Basu has a diploma in Production Management. So that is now considered essential for the position of a Production Supervisor. The fact that Basu was giving a good performance even before he started studies for the diploma is conveniently overlooked. Patel is a chartered accountant and Rao is a cost and works accountant. So for administrative positions, chartered accountants get preference. Nobody has looked into the curriculum of the two examinations to see if this is justified.

We have no clear idea as to what to look for in providing personnel for a specific post. We have no way of appraising whether a person has the internal characteristics we feel we should look for. So we ask for external characteristics we can appraise, however irrelevant they may be.

The army is the oldest organisation in the world. The procedures used in army recruitment are characteristic of this expedient way of tackling the problem of providing personnel. Do we know what makes a good soldier or a good officer? The army has been stressing the physical dimensions in selecting soldiers. That probably had some relevance in the days when the lance was the main weapon and reach was of some importance. However, the discovery of gunpower obsoleted lance and in effect "cut all soldiers to the same height." Yet the physical dimensions continue to figure in the selection procedure even centuries after gunpowder invention, so that the fact that nuclear warfare possibilities are not even considered in the present selection procedure should not be surprising. Similarly, the leadership ideas of the army have been completely discredited in the behavioural science research in the last 30 years: but the army continues to base its selection of officers on its stone age theories of leadership.

## WHAT WE CAN GET...

In certain cases, our personnel policies for getting people for jobs seems to be governed by what we can get for the money than by what we require for the job. Here are two interesting cases:

Company A used to advertise clerical positions in accounting mentioning "A.C.A. or A.C.W.A preferred." Due to the fairly adequate salary offered and lack of opportunities elsewhere for such accountants, the company got about 10 accountants in their clerical staff. When the market for accounants picked up, 7 of them left for better opportunities elsewhere. Out of the remaining 3, 2 are incompetent and the third cannot get a job elsewhere because of his offensive mannerism. Now the company is stuck with these problems:

1.  Three unsatisfactory employees, who are frustrated and have a grievance that their work is far below their qualifications.

2.  Difficulty in getting new recruits in the clerical staff as the Personnal Department is unwilling to reduce the qualifications for the posts.

3.  Difficulty in attracting new qualified accountants as the state of the present qualified persons discourages new applicants.

Company B got science graduates as plant operators because of the salary offered. When these graduates got experience, they left for supervisory positions elsewhere. So the company decided to take only under-graduates for the operators jobs. However, it did not want to lower the qualifications too much. So it advertised for inter science passed candidates. Since any good calibre inter science

40

passed student goes for graduation, the Company got really third-rate staff consisting of those who somehow got through inter science, but could not pass the graduate exmaination.

## PROMOTION-A SIMPLER WAY?

Another way of getting people for jobs is by promoting from within the organisation. At first, this seems a simpler way as you are supposed to know a person working in the organisation much better than the outsider you have to judge in a short interview. In practice, however, it has turned out to be an extremely complex problem mainly because:

We do not know exactly what the job requires.

We do not know exactly what the person has.

So naturally we are not sure if the person is best suited for that job (and vice versa).

In order to determine what a job requires, a few companies have carried out the enormous task of writing position objectives and position descriptions for every job so that at least the output of the job is cleary defined. However, whenever the next step of determining the attributes essential to give that output e.g. verbal, arithmetical and analytical aspects of aptitude, social and creative abilities, imagination, etc. is attempted, we come across a strange phenomenon. The attributes essential are rated so high that the accounts assistant can straight walk into a managing director's position.

The appraisal of current employees is generally so subjective and unsystematic, that the word 'merit' has acquired a strange meaning. In discussion with an enlgihtened trade union leader, I commented upon the adherence to seniority generally advocated by the unions disregarding merit. He admitted freely the drawbacks of the union's attitude, but pointed out the confusion regarding merit. "Through the centuries," he remarked, "many have listed the defects of the marriage system. But the system is going strong, because nobody has found an alternative for organised sex relations and family formation. Similarly, unless a good alternative is found, seniority will continue to be the criterion that gives a feeling of fairness and confidence "

A few companies have instituted a system of committee-appraisals to get a systematic and objective evaluation of current employees. While this is a great improvement over a situation comprising either an absence of appraisals or an unsystematic appraisal by the immediate superior alone, it still leaves much to be desired. In many instances, it is the immediate superior who virtually does all the appraisal—other members politely nodding their heads. Very often there is a real confusion as to what is being appraised and the weightage given to the various aspects of the job. What is more important: Doing the job exactly the way the boss wants, or in a way that shows imagination and creativity? Getting things done even treading on somebody's corns, or keeping people happy even if it delays or otherwise affects the job to be done? The appraisal committee members are rarely trained in the system, so each has his own viewpoint. Thus, the system often leads to a drill rather than to an appraisal. The forms are somehow filled in and sent away.

In some systems, a post-appraisal interview with the person appraised is included. It is surprising how many managers avoid this interview and sometimes make even a false report on the post-appraisal interview. Some managers just scrape through by mentioning good aspects and giving a general pious sermon.

Thus, the system of using merit for promotions is not likely to give a sense of fairness and confidence unless considerable efforts are spent on:

Finding out the attributes required for a post.

Appraising, as objectively as possible, the attributes of the current employees.

## CURRENT PRACTICES IN PROMOTION

Since most companies do not spend efforts in this direction, the current practices in promotion may be summed up as:

1. Simple seniority system in which you relax and wait for your turn. This is often called the 'Government System'.

2. Unspecified vague system which is supposed to consider merit as the criterion, sometimes, to make it more complicated, with some 'weightage' for seniority. This is known as the 'Ulcar System'.

3. In expanding companies, everybody gets promoted sooner or later unless he is involved in malpractice, insubordination, etc. So all you have to do is to keep your noselean and wait for the tide. This is called the 'Tide System'.

4. Some companies feel diffident about evaluating their own staff. So they wait till the brighter boys apply elsewhere and are selected for a better job. Then they dissuade them from leaving by offering promotion. This is called the 'Blackmail System'

5. In army, each post has a certain specified age limit. If the person does not go to a higher post before reaching the age limit, he is retired. This is known as 'Up-or-Out System'.

## HOW TO PROMOTE WITHOUT REALLY PROMOTING

All this analysis is valid as long as the real intention is to promote a person. However, there are instances when the management does not desire to promote but is forced to. A survey has revealed that the following are the most popular methods:

1. **Change-the-label Method**: This is the least expensive method. The other day, I got a visiting card from an Area Manager of an office equipment company.

43

When I called him into my office, I found a very young-looking man. So I asked him how he rose upto such a high position so early and what was the scope and area of his operation. He told me that this was the lowest position they had. He had joined only a month ago after passing Senior Cambridge in the third attempt. He was in charge of sales of the visual index system in the area: 21, Chowringheee to 58, Chowringhee! This has been adopted by many more prestigious organisations like advertising agencies and banks in U.S.A. which have scores of vice-presidents. In India, I understand, the Indian Standards Institute calls its lowest technical position: Extra-Assistant Director!

Thus, any person can be given a feeling of promotion by changing the label of his post though this may not increase his responsibilities. In some cases, the change is made more impressive by changing some external working conditions e.g. putting up a partition around the person or raising an existing partition to a little extra height. This reminds me of an interesting Gujarati couplet:

Tane kone kahi didhu maranani baad mukti chhe

Rahe chhe kaida enie, fakat diwal badle chhe.

(Who told you there is freedom after death? The imprisonment remains the same, only the walls change!)

2. **Promote-all-god's-children Method**: Psychologically, promotion is relative. So by promoting everybody, you promote nobody! This system is eminently suitable for a demotion. If you promote everybody except one, that one is automatically demoted without your having to announce the difficult demoting decision.

3. **Change-the-place Method**: If you transfer A to B's position and B to A's position, you can meet them separately and congratulate both on their promotion. The success of the system obviously depends upon your ability to insulate A from B.

44

4. **Second-to-none-announcement Method:** The late President Kennedy introduced a system in his announcement of appointments which is worthy of emulation. In his announcement, he described every appointment as "second to none in its importance..." Can we look forward to an announcment transferring a Branch Manager to the Head of Mail Section, Head Office as a momentous posting giving him responsibilities "second to none in importance...?"

5. **Strip-the-job Method**: In this system, the post to which the person is being promoted is stripped off-reducing its responsibilities, authority, etc. Thus, instead of promoting the man, you demote the position!

## CONCLUSION

Promotion is an important tool for motivating the employees. However, the way promotions are handled, they seem to lead mostly to frustration, scepticism and bickering.

# five faces of
# indian managers:

THERE are many factors which seem to limit the tempo of India's economic development. Scarcity of financial resources, equipment, foreign exchange, skilled personnel, etc: are often cied as the main causes. However, when one looks at the actual working of industrial enterprises, both in private and public sectors, one finds wastage of financial resources in high inventories or delayed projects, wastage of equipment in idle capacities even where the products are in scarcity, wastage of foreign exchange by tardy import subsituation and wastage of skilled personnel by unimaginative placements.

Thus it seems that behind the facade of these scarcities lies the real scarcity—scarcity of management talent. A vague realisation of this scarcity has led to so-called management development programmes. Management development is now developing so fast that it seems to be the development to end all developments. Right from half-day seminars that end with lunch (beer on the house in non-dry locations) to three-month residential courses that end with gala dinners, there is a continual management development spree.

So a time has come to find out what is the management that is being developed in India. Who are these managers that are supposed to put in practice modern management concepts like delegation, participation, leadership, management by exception, managment by results, etc, etc. India is a country with many religions, many languages many parties and an increasing number of states So it is not surprising that we have many types of managers.

Looking for unity in diversity, most of our managers may be classified into five major groups, viz:

A. The feudal vizir

B. The jack of all trades

C. The over-promoted headclerk

D. The cocktail manager

E. The babe in the woods

It may be emphasised here that this classification still leaves some managers out. Furthermore, the managers considered are employees in the mangement cadre—and not owners, proprietors or entrepreneurs.

## THE FEUDAL VIZIR

This species is found in concerns popularly known as family concerns. In a typical situation, a family member is in charge of a group of concerns and he has a manager— often known as his right-hand or left-hand or left-hand man. The manager has actually a designation at times— like General Manager or Technical Adviser. But quite often he is simply known as Shri Nandiji through whom you have to approach Seth Shankarji.

The vizir type of manager holds his office entirely at the pleasure of the sultan. Consequently, the sultan's confidence rather than the vizir's competence is the basis of authority. Personal loyalty, rather than integrity, is the main qualification. At times, the vizir is expected to get into or carry on somewhat shady deals for the personal benefit of the sultan.

The vizir in turn has his own sub-vizirs or subedars who hold a similar relationship to him. Thus, the whole organisation gets built-up like the Mughal court. In extreme cases, darbars are held periodically, which the subordinates are expected to attend to show their complete subservience to their overlords

50

The modern management concepts like delegation, participation, management by objectives, by exception or by results have very little scope in such organisations. Authority delegation is based on personal relationship rather than on job requirements. The whole organisation is often oriented towards the personal benefit of the sultan rather than towards an overall objective relevant to the progress of the organisation. Results are judged subjectively; star-gazing is resorted to more often than objective data and systematic decision-making procedures.

## THE JACK OF ALL TRADERS

The vizir of the private sector seems to appear in a slighly different guise in the public sector. At the very start of the public sector enterprise, the inherent power in the top managerial position in the industry attracted the attention of our civil service. As the proverb goes "When a blind man distributes sweets, he gives his own kith and kin." Similarly, the civil service dominating . the rarified atmosphere of New Delhi managed to convert itself overnight into a tribe of industrial managers competent in every field of industrial activity and allocated the new positions to themselves.

The situation has been further aggravated by the extraordinary hunger of this tribe. An ordinary mortal would be satisfied with one important job But these individual of rare competence generally manage to occupy a number of offices simultaneously. If you think that the Chairmanship of such a complex enterprise as the Indian Airlines would be a full-time job for an individual, you are wrong. The indiviaul could be, in adition, the Secretary of the Ministry of Civil Aviation, Member of the Administrative Reforms Commission and Special Officer for Reorganisation of services between Punjab and Haryana—not to count the membership of several committees.

51

Those who complain about services rendered by public sector enterprises should do well to remember that they should be thankful that some services get rendered occasionally. When a dog walks on his hind legs, we clap not because he walks well but because he walks at all With the civil administrators who have converted themselves overnight into industrial managers in all sectors of industrial activity, not much can be expected in the way of scientific, systematic or modern management With the jacks of all trades managing the trade, we are fortunate to have any trade left at all.

## THE OVER-PROMOTED HEAD-CLERK

After having looked at some of the managers in Indian-managed private and public sectors, let us look at the managers in the so-called foreign-managed concerns.

There are many ways of observing Indpendence Day— from the usual flag-hoisting to the waving of black flags with or without throwing stones at the police or railway staff. One of my friends who is a manager in a foreign concern observes the Indpendence Day in a peculiar way. He goes to his office in spite of the holiday—and sits at the head-clerk's desk for 10 minutes to meditate. His explanation is: but for independence, he would have ended there.

In the bad old days, in many foreign managed concerns Indians were not expected to rise beyond a particular level—usually the head-clerk level—and higher levels were manned by imports. With independence, import-substitution in management ranks became inevitable and many employees recruited to become head-clerks suddenly found themselves in managerial chairs.

The stresses and strains of over-promotion are evident when you meet these managers. An obvious characteristic is their habit of referring to the management as "they" These managers do not feel part of the management. Even when these persons rise to the top management level, they are diffident to assume authority and find every excuse to pass the buck. Thus, in many foreign concerns, when the foreigners left the top management positions to Indians, they took away the top management authority with themselves and the organisations virtually became puppet-shows.

## THE COCKTAIL MANAGER

Another type of manager so characteristic of foreign-managed concerns is the one that excels in cocktail parties. He is selected by that strange process of recruitment which is governed by the Law of Decreasing Calibre. The law states: if third-rate persons are selecting, the probability of selection of third-rate and fourth-rate persons is about equal and approaches the value 0.5. The selectors are suspicious of the second-rate candidates and they find the first-raters simply crazy.

Since the calibre is at such a disadvantage and since the number of third-rate and fourth-rate candidates is very large, the factors determining selection are the superficial ones—e.g., dress, accent, family connections, etc. The persons so selected specialise in nothing, but an overall outward smartness and their greatest asset is their capacity for holding alcohol.

In the process of time, such managers form the selections panel and select their own types—thus perpetuating the cult of cocktail managers. To these managers, management is a process of "getting alone" with other similar managers and holding their own at various intra-company and inter-company cocktail parties.

While the process of perpetuation of the cult is obvious, there are two theories about the origin of the cult. According to the first theory, such managers were purposely chosen by the foreigners so as to avoid having too smart Indians in their management cadres—which seemed reasonable in the days when top management positions were always filled by imports. According to the other theory, the foreigners slecting the cocktail managers were themselves somewhat of the same type —the export of first-raters from "Home" having declined due to increasing opportunities at Home and decreasing attractiveness of a career in India.

## THE BABE IN THE WOODS

To this last category belong the recruits who have come fresh with formal management education from universities in India or abroad. They are looking forward to apply all the latest techniques they have just learnt.

In the management jungle, these babes go through the heart-breaking process of disillusionment. Nobody in the purchase department seems to have heard of the "economic order quantity". The sales department cannot make head or tail of "exponential smoothening of demand forecast". The costing system, where it exists, is the good old historical absorption costing system and marginal costing is Greek and Latin to the costing department.

To work with the organisation, these babes have to unlearn and come down to the general sophistication level of the organisation. It is interesting to note that many organisations probably spend as much money to untrain these newcomers as to train the old-timers.

## CONCLUSION

These five faces probably cover about 90 per cent of our managers. Any expenditure on management development of these managers is a doubtful investment. In the field of education, one of the basic concepts is: if you want to teach Johnny arithmetic—you must know not only arithmetic, you must also know Johnny. Any attempt to develop management in India must take into account not only the latest techniques of developing in the management field, but also the types of Indian managers and the working mangement environment in India.

# SEVEN

# management
# by crisis

YEARS ago, when I started my career as a consultant, I was fascinated by an executive who seemed to be in the habit of tearing off nearly half his mail. One morning I was witnessing his extra-quick mail disposal system and I could not resist asking him why he was filing a considerable portion of his mail in the wastepaper basket.

"I am responsible for office furniture and equipment sanctions and these are all indents for bookcases and two-drawer filing cabinets.:

"But why destroy them?" I asked.

"Every joker who lays his hands on a reference book feels he must have a bookcase; if he gets hold of a couple of 'confidential' files, he needs a filing cabinet. If we give everybody what he asks for, we shall have the office overflowing with bookcases which will hold mostly stationery and other junk as well as filing cabinets which will have little else besides tennis shoes."

"But suppose somebody *really* needs a bookcase of a filing cabinet?"

"Then he will write me a reminder; then a second reminder. Ultimately he will walk to my office and drag me along to show how books are piled on the floor and files are stuffed in his drawers. That is the time to consider his indent.'

As I was young, I did not realise that I was witnessing an example of 'management by crisis'—which has been playing an increasing role in various sectors of our life.

## INDIGENOUS KNOW-HOW

We are importing a lot of know-how for our industrial growth. At the same time, we are emphasising that real industrialisation can come only through our own indigenous know-how. But we seem to neglect the opportunity to promote and export such indigenous know-how when it is available.

For example, we have been importing the phrase; 'management by committee', 'management by objectives', 'management by results', 'management by techniques', 'management by exception', etc., etc. We talk a lot about these various types of managements. But we do not publicise the major management style we practise i.e. 'management by crisis'—which has been developed so well by us right on the Indian soil!

It is high time we recognise this type of management and understand its potential.

## HOW TO MANAGE BY CRISIS

For the beginners to recognise and practise management by crisis, the following elementary rules would be useful:

1. **Do not recognise a problem—unless a crisis develops:** "... what do you mean by 'quality of canteen food is bad? You have heard the workers grumbling? So what? I have been grumbling about my wife's cooking for years—when she is out of ear-shot. That means nothing. If the workers are really unhappy, they will have a tool-down strike and then we shall do something about it..."

2. **If possible, shift the crisis:** "... the second shift workers are protesting because they have to leave so late that they can get no transport? Then advance the shift timings by one hour so that they will leave one hour earlier... Yes, that would mean that the first shift chaps will have to come one hour earlier... How can we

be sure that they will have no transport to come to work? Let's announce the new timings and cross the bridge when we come to it..."

3. **In case of a crisis, look for a temporary solution:** It is important to see that the problem is somehow suppressed since solving it may rob us of continual crises in the future.

"... The blowroom workers are on strike because of excessive dust nuisance. O.K., offer them a goggle and mask set each. I am sure they would like the goggles... I know they would find the mask uncomfortable, but then it might be rather difficult and costly to seal the ducts and change the exhaust fans..."

## HOW TO GENERATE A CRISIS

In the management by crisis system, every executive knows that his value to management is determined by the magnitude of crisis in the area. This is historically known as Malharrao Holkar philosophy—after the grand old man who advised Dattolji Scindia before the Third War of Panipat 'not to destroy all the enemies—otherwise the overlords (Peshwas) will have no use for us'

Some managers are lucky to have a readymade crisis. But for others it might be necessary to start from the raw and develop their own crisis. In such cases, the following suggestions might prove helpful:

1. **Time-the-great-creator Approach:** If you neglect a small problem long enough, it can develop into a first class crisis.

"Pilots have stopped flying planes for want to blankets?... Yes, we received their demand two years ago When we received a reminder six months after that, we put it on the agenda of the Grievance Committee, which discussed it in three meetings in the next six months. We called for quotations a year ago and forwarded them to the Chairman for sanction through proper channels six months ago. We got the sanction last months and we are now ready to purchase—but these pilots have no patience..."

2. **We-have-our-rules Approach:** Any problem constantly confronted by rigid rules can develop into a crisis. "Workers want their overall 6" longer! We can't do that as the rule specifically states that they will get $4^{1/2'}$ long overalls... They may have been shrunk by the dhobi, but if we have to give the cloth for stitching after shrinking, I must get a specific directive from the Policy Committee..."

3. **Keep-them-in-their-place Approach:** If you treat people badly enough, you will have no shortage of crisis.

"Ram has submitted a proposal to shift the cycle-stand so that cycles would be in the shade instead of in the sun. Who is this Ram to put up such proposals? What does he think of himself? Is he the manger or am I? The only way to keep these chaps in their place is to bang them as soon as they open their mouths..."

4. **Tough-talk-with-wobbly-knees Approach:** If you can talk tough, but cannot get your employees to believe in your toughness, you will have no difficulty in getting a crisis.

"You must not leave your place of work. I don't care whether you are thirsty or hungry... May be you can go twice to the toilet, but that is the limit... smoking break can be allowed not more than thrice in a shift... If somebody is having a definite headache, he can sit out not more than five minutes at a time..."

5. **Give-him-cake Approach:** If you appease an aggression, you can be sure of a continual crisis. There is a story of a boy who returned from school with a black eye.

"What happened?" asked his mother. "The class bully hit me," said the boy. "Well, it might be a good idea to make friends with him. Take a piece of cake for him tomorrow." The next day the boy returned with the other eye blackened. "What happened?" asked his mother. "The bully hit me again", replied the boy, "he wants more cake."

## ADVANTAGES OF MANAGEMENTS BY CRISIS

As noted earlier, the main advantage of management by crisis is that mangers can retain their value. If the running becomes very smooth, there is a tendency amongst some top managements to assume that the job can be done by anybody ("even my young nephew can manage this department"—and if it is a family-managed concern, the nephew may really get in as a replacement). On the other hand, if there are recurring major crisis situations, not only will the manager be considered irreplaceable—but he may also be treated as a person with increasing value. Crisis may help managers to show their mettle. As the saying goes: "When the going gets tough, the tough get going."

Another advantage is the reduction of workload—at least in the initial stages—since no problem is accepted unless it becomes a crisis, a lot of problems are not faced at all.

Management by crisis also gives a manager a feeling of achievement. In a smoothly run departmnet, the manager gets bored by the time the day is half over. The crisis manager has no lack of excitement. When he returns home an hour and a half late, he can impress his wife with a brief descritpion of "today's crisis" and get her sympathy. On the other hand, a non-crisis managers may receive from his wife.

"Your just go to the office at 9 in the morning and are back by 5 in the evening. There is no substance in you, nothing happens to you. You and your campany are

61

just useless. Look at my friend Lakshmi's husband.
There is always something going on in his company.
They had four gheraos in the last three months. He
goes early at 7 in the morning and there is no
guarantee whether he will return at 9 in the evening
or at midnight. When she talks about her husband in
our Club, I have to just keep mum and listen..."

## EXPANDING HORIZONS

The philosophy of management by crisis has spread far
beyond the field of industrial management. It has been so
much evident in government work that some believe that
it was originated by the government and was brought into
the industry through the public sector.

It has infiltrated itself into the academic world and seeped
up the ivory towers. It has got into every aspect of our life.
Marriage by crisis, children by crisis, education by crisis,
job by crisis, work by crisis and even death by crisis are
the characteristics of modern India. Even our cricketers
seem to play better in a crisis—which they generate so
often.

The following are some recent examples of the expanding
horizons of this philosophy:

'**Municipal corporations:** In Calcutta, the
Conservancy Department of the Municipal Corporation
is in a continual crisis. Out of 250 corporation lorries,
more than 100 are lying idle because of "lack of spare
parts," although arrangements have been made for
cash purchase of these parts. The situation is further
accentuated by frequent 'lightning strikes of the
conservancey workers—they had 36 such strikes in one
year!

'**Hospitals:** In the Kanchrapara T.B. Hospital (west
Bengal) nearly 100 patients are occupying beds since a
number of years despite discharge notices. At least 18

of these have been certified fit to return home and work—but have contunued to live in the hospital for more than 5 years. The oldest case is of a patient who has been living in the hospital since 1949. The patients have formed an association called "Arogyakami Kalyan Samity" (Committee for the Welfare of the Health-weekers). This association gheraoed and manhandled the Superintendent of the Hospital demanding increased supply of rice. A hospital sweeper was assaulted by one of these patients and in protest the hospital staff refused to work. The patients demonstrated against this and damaged furniture worth Rs 3,000.

'**Prisons:** In Muzaffarpur (Bihar) 400 prisoners armed with spears and choppers held noisy demonstrations demanding better food. Bihar's Jail Minister intervened and assured them that he would look into their grievances. He also announced two months remission in their period of sentence.

'**Schools and Colleges:** Schools and Colleges all over India many a time have a continual crisis. In Madras as well as some other places the students fight in out periodically with the bus workers. In Cuttack the Medical College students clashed with the employees of the hospital. In North Bengal and Indore, two colleges clashed and created serious law and order problem. In Coimbatore, students burnt the national flag and generally made things upleasant. With this education, the students should do well as Crisis Managers in their future vocations.

## SOME PROBLEMS WITH MANAGEMENT BY CRISIS

The famous playgirl actress Zsa Zsa Gabor was asked, "Do you accept gifts from perfect strangers?"

"No" she replied, "I do not accept gifts from perfect strangers. But then, who is perfect in this world?"

Similarly, management by crisis—though admirable in many ways—is not a perfect philosophy. Its wide-scale applications have revealed some shortcomings.

The first problem in the management by crisis approach is that the definition of 'crisis' keeps changing. There was a time when a procession causing two hours traffic jam on Howrah Bridge with a few hundred people missing their trains, etc. used to make a front page column in local papers. Today, it barely gets a mention in the inside pages. In fact, unless there are a few persons killed, an agitation just cannot rate the front page. "Our editor has instructed us", a sub-editor told me, "unless a dozen people are killed, don't give it a headline." The other day, the *Statesman* had to combine student riots in three places to give a headline on the front page. In the good old days, any one of them would have been a starred item.

Secondly, people are getting so accustomed to creating a crisis that they are creating them without the existence of any problem. Recently, the Nagpur University had to abandon the Convocation Ceremony because of a student demonstration. When the reporters asked the reason for the demonstration, they found that some students wanted to "remove Hindi" while some others wanted to "remove English." In fact, the University had the certificates in Marathi—so neither Hindi nor English was involved.

The crises are becoming increasingly costly. In my younger days, I took a minor part in the 1942 crisis. I threw four stones and broke a municipal lamp with the last one. I was looking forward to relating this incident to my grand-children to boast about my destructive brave young days. But by now things have already changed. A damage worth a few lakhs of rupees is carried out in a fair-sized city even before breakfast. A simple incident in Assam on the Republic Day caused greater damage than the whole 1942 movement that we were so proud of a generation ago. I can very well imagine my grand-children telling me:

"We had a difficult paper on Economics, so we are asking the University to get everybody passed—otherwise we shall have to blow up the DVC Dams.. just like the Bhakra-Nangal Dam blown up by the Punjab students because the University did not allow a larger space to the Student Union... it is no longer possible to create a crisis to get action just by blowing a power station; the Madras Electricity Company clerical staff did that to remove the computers installed in the company. It did not work so well although the whole city was without power and the computer could not work anyway... In these days except dams there is nothing else we can blow up, since most of the rail lines, railway stations and wagons were blown up by the last generation. In fact they left us so little to blow up..."

Lastly, if the crises grow in size—and in number—we may not be able to manage them at all. Then there is no management by crisis left. What is left is crisis leading to bankruptcy.

# the problem of
# illiterate managers

THERE is a story of two men one young and one old who were travelling by train. When the train stopped at a station, the old man asked the young man. "What is the name of this station?" The young man looked out, saw the name-board right opposite the window and replied: "This is Kharagpur Station; can you not read that board?" The old man peered out and muttered, "No", "Well, I think I can do something about it", said the young man, "I am an optician". So he opened his brief-case and took out several pairs of spectacles. The old man tried them one after another, but still could not read the name-board. "This is indeed an interesting case", said the optician, "however, since you are also going to Calcutta, you better come to my consulting room on Park Street tomorrow and I shall see how I can get you to read". "That is indeed kind of you" said the man, "but in all fairness I must tell you I never learnt to read!"

The gigantic efforts undertaken by various training institutes to train out managers in utilising modern techniques often makes me wonder whether we are providing spectacles to illiterates, hoping they will be able to read just by using the spectacles.


## THE BASIC MANAGEMENT

This brings us to the concept of literacy of managers i.e. understanding of basic management. The word "management" is being defined or described constantly mostly by professors using words which are often more difficult to understand. To me, it seems possible to describe management through three simple concepts: Accountability, Trust and System.

Accountability is the responsibility for achieving some specific organisational objectives. The concept involves setting of specific objectives and a periodic appraisal of performance vis-a-vis the objectives. Where accountability does not exist, there is no management possible and the managers in such organisations are mere vagrants under glorified titles. The situation regarding some of our public sector enterprises may be examined from this viewpoint. The distinction between accountability for results and accountability for procedures must be emphasised at this stage. In public sector operations, a person's accountability is often defined by the procedures and not by the results. As long as the prcedures laid down are followed a person can have the "Gita attitude" of not worrying about the results. So, many a man works diligently to put his 'notes' on the file to protect himself rather than to achieve any specific results. Thus the people seem to work for the futures i.e., for the audit and investigation committees that will prepare their reports after many years, rather than for the present to support production or sales. This is obviously a form of illiteracy spread on a massive scale in our managerial class.

The manager does not work by himself. He works with his colleagues, subordinates and superiors. In fact, the effectiveness of a manager depends upon his ability to work as a team and to get the work done through the team. This involves "trust" in subordinates, superiors and colleagues. Yet there are several instances of managers refusing to trust. They do not delegate authority to their subordinates; they depend on a 'departmental spy' system and on cliques against colleagues or superiors. This is another form of illiteracy prevalent amongst our managers.

A distinguishing characteristic of managerial work is decisions. A manager takes decision himself, as well as

70

evaluates the decisions taken by his subordinates, colleagues and superiors. To use intuition or hunch for the formation or evaluation of decisions is another form of illiteracy. A 'literate' manager institutes systems, i.e. determines the information essential to take the decision and establishes the channel to get this information in time.

## THE ORIGIN AND RISE OF ILLITERATE MANAGERS

It may be interesting to see how we got so many illiterate managers some of them even at the highest level. This would take us to the origin of our Indian managers and here we see three distinct streams: The first is the 'Feudal Stream' consisting of the managers who initially started as zamindars' agents and moved into industry when their feudal lords became industrial entrepreneurs. This stream can now be seen in the so-called family concerns. Here the managers could hardly acquire any literacy since many of the entrepreneurs, though admirable in their vision and strategy were themselves illiterates in managerial requirements. The organisations were generally inbred and insulated against external sophistication.

The second is the 'Government Stream' consisting of civil service and military. This class of officers was created by a foreign power basically to maintain law and order and to protect their rule. As such they were never trained for the managerial jobs in industrial enterprises. With the advent of the public sector, these officers overnight became industrial managers, but remained illiterate in the managerial requirements.

The third stream is the 'Foreign Stream' consisting of subsidiaries of foreign companies. For a long time the managerial group in these organisations was imported and there was very little need for us Indians to get sophisticated. Suddenly, independence came and we were pushed into a managerial position without getting any

71

time to understand the managerial requirements, very often the superficial aspects e.g. dress, accent, golf, liquor, etc. were taken as the essential managerial requirements with no attention to accountability, trust and system.

In the protected market in the post-independence era, these managers flourished. The organisations grew due to greater economic opportunities in spite of these illiterate managers and the managers strutted around claiming the credit.

## THE DECLINE AND FALL OF ILLITERATE MANAGERS

Then came the recession of 1967 and the stuffing started falling out. The straw inside the grey flannel suit is becoming only too evident. Many family concerns are finding their growth severely limited by the managers they collected around themselves and kept illiterate over these years. The public sector is finding itself the object of ridicule.

Recently, a Japanese delegation visiting one of our biggest public sector factories refused to believe that India is poor. "No poor country can afford to keep an investment of 250 crores utilized at 10 per cent capacity!" they exclaimed. Many foreign subsidiaries are finding it difficult to maintain their profitability in a competitive market and are finding it easiest to dispose of managers as 'surplus' since their contribution sems to be negligible.

## THE FUTURE

Obviously, we cannot afford to live with managerial illiteracy or with any other illiteracy if we have to progress. Gunnar Myrdal in his recent work 'Asian Drama' has emphasised that the condition of 'under-development' is a total condition pervading the entire society. For a sustained movement towards modernisation, major changes are required in all aspects including the fundamental attitudes of the people towards each other and towards work itself. Without such basic changes the drive towards modernisation will flounder and the society will develop 'softness' i.e. lack of discipline that is required to carry out the necessary radical programmes. The evidence of softness is the great gap between the ambitious statements in the plans and the actual implementation of the plans to facilitate economic development and modernisation.

An important reason for the softness is the illiteracy of our managers. Unless they harden themselves they would find themselves incapable of effective participation in our economic progress in fact, they are likely to retard the process.

## CONCLUSION

So it is imperative that we tackle the problem of illiterate managers on a priority basis. Train we must, but the training should be aimed at the basic problem of management. The training to institute accountability, trust and system should have priority.When the basic management is firmly established, the application of modern techniques is greatly facilitated and the usual frustration amongst the technique-trained personnel, who find the application of techniques barred by the illiterate managers, can be avoided.

The situation is desperate and calls for speedy action—an adult education campaign to tackle the problem of illiterate managers.

# the technique of
# defensive management

THERE is a story of a man who helped a Minister and requested something in return.

"What do you want?" asked the Minister.

"I want to be a postmaster," replied the man.

"But you can neither read nor write. How can you work in a post office?" asked the Minister.

"Who is talking of work? I don't want to be an assistant postmaster. I want to be a postmaster," insisted the man.

The man had grasped the essentiais of defensive management. To work hard and rish high in the management is a technique widely known though not so widely practised. But not to work hard and rise higher in the management, i.e. the technique of defensive management, has been deliberately hidden by interested parties and it has taken considerable research to bring out the essentials of this technique.

## POWER IS TROUBLE—SO IDENTIFY THE POWER

The first principle of defensive management is: "Keep your nose clean". This is not an advertisement for handkerchiefs. It simply means: Keep out of trouble.

Very few people deliberately plan to get into trouble. Most people get into trouble because they inadvertantly get foul of the "Power"—i.e. people who have the authority to make or mar their careers.

77

This means you must identify the 'Power'. Normally, you may consider your boss to be the first level of power and go through him upwards to higher levels of power. But this rule might prove misleading. In a family concern, the nephew of the Sethji is Power though he may be just a colleague—or even a subordinate. This is particularly true if he is staying with the Sethji and the latter is in the habit of enquiring about office affairs at dinner. Similarly, in a foreign-managed concern, the person who knows somebody "back Home" can be formidable—far beyond his level.

So how can a newcomer identify th 'Power'—or even an old-timer recognise when the power shifts? In feudal days, kings wore crowns and the bigger the king, bigger was his crown. In the army, levels are revealed by the amount of brass carried. In industrial concerns, such visible signs of power are not common. Organisation charts are most likely to lead you astray. Sometimes the higher levels in the charts are manned by persons who are marking time for retirement and have no 'say' in what is going on. It is much safer to talk to old-timers and keep your eyes and ears open to observe who is running the show.

One rule given by our sages is "follow the big men" i.e. observe who are the people the seniors are currying favour with. However, our research has led us to a simpler rule: In a company party, observe how the executives' wives form a cluster. The centre of the cluster is the wife of the Top Power. Power diminishes as the square of the distance from the wife of the Top Power. This is because women are more ruthless than men and when power shifts, they physically elbow out the wife of the executive who has lost power and put her in her proper place.

## STICK CLOSE TO POWER

Once you have identified the power, the next step is to stay close to it. It seems paradoxical that to stay away from trouble, you should stay near the Power which means trouble. However, this does not seem so paradoxical when you consider that the best way to keep from getting run over by a car is to sit in the car.

To stay close to Power, it is essential to observe these rules:

1. **Conform**: Dress as those in power do. If they wear grey suits, white shirts with dark ties, you do the same. If they wear blue suits, yellow shirts and green ties, you wear blue suits, green shirts and yellow ties. Similarly, talk as they do; join the same club; play the same games. It is a waste of time to improve your tennis when the top is busy playing golf. Read the same papers that the Power reads so that you can respond intelligently.

2. **Listen**: People in power are great talkers. They can talk both for you and for themselves. Remember, nobody has listened himself out of a promotion. So just listen. You can make up for the silence when you come into power.

3. **Drink**: Within your limits. For reasons unknown, there is a great admiration in management circles towards persons who have a large capacity for alcohol i.e. who can drink without getting drunk (although this seems a waste of costly alcohol). However, if you have to move on four alien feet at the end of every party, your reputation is likely to be adversely affected.

4. **Stay**: At a proper 'address'/ After all, Judges Court Road in Calcutta is just an extension of Hazra Road and Chowringhee is more or less an extension of Russa Road yet the address makes all the difference.

## HOW TO DEAL WITH COMPETITION

When you start sticking close to the Power, you may suddenly find that you are not alone. The place near the Power is always crowded and you have to face competition.

79

You may be tempted to underrate the competition and steamroll over them. Don't try that. You will have everybody against you and, most likely, you will be steamrolled. Have patience. Analyse the competition. Find out their strong points (including family connections) and respect them. Even when somebody in the crowd is obviously slipping don't push him back (leave your wife to elbow his wife out), don't step on him, step over him.

You cannot beat competition physically. You can beat it only by specific aspects of the defensive management technique. These aspects are:

1. **Be in the 'Know'**: Knowledge about Power is power of the second order. If you can know the shift of power in advance, you can beat others and get close to the New Power before others get there. This means keeping yourself right onto the grapevine. In every office there is a Rumour Exchange. You patronise this Exchange and occasionally feed it with intelligent rumours of your own creation so that you can get preferential treatment.

2. **Be 'Visible'**: Join every activity that leads to the power. This way you can increase your chances of being near the power when the competition is absent. At least, you will be seen by the Power.

3. **Be 'Amorphous'**: Try to create an impression about yourself which is generally favourable without being anything definite.

## HOW TO DEAL WITH YOUR BOSS

Barring exceptional circumstances, your approach to the Power will have to be largely through your boss. So it is vital to understand your boss. By and large, bosses can be classified into the following three categories.

1. **The Promotable**: This is the best type of boss to have. Often, the Power is waiting for adequate

replacement to move the man up—and you can be the replacement.

2. **The Caretaker:** This man may be too old in age—or otherwise too obsolete—to move up. However, he can be replaced if an attractive replacement is available.

3. **The Static**: This is the worst type of boss to have. He is not old enough to be considered for retirement and is competent enough to keep on holding his job. But he is not 'promotable'. So he will stay where he is—and so will you if you are in his hold.

The techniques to deal with the three types of bosses are obviously different. With the promotable boss, you stick close to him and hang on his coat-tails so that when he moves up you move up. As far as you are concerned, he is the king-maker and you please him to get ahead.

When you are under a caretaker boss you must find out who is the kingmaker for your level. Rarely does the caretaker boss determine his successor. The kingmaker is generally on the next higher level and you have to aim at him.

With a static boss, the only way you can move is around him. Getting a transfer to another boss is the logical method—but this will take a lot of tact. You cannot go to your boss and tell him, "I want a transfer because you are not likely to get anywhere". You may have to go out and "sell" yourself to other departments so that you are asked for by one of the promotable (or caretaker) bosses.


## HOW TO PLEASE THE KINGMAKER

So ultimately you are under a kingmaker or under a nominal (caretaker) boss and have identified your kingmaker. This is not all. There might be others in the same situation and you have to race ahead of them to qualify.

There are eight ways to please the kingmaker:

1. **Be loyal to him:** Support him, boost him, his work and his record. Do not be critical of him or cast aspersions on him. See that he comes to know about this and he will note that.

2. **Agree with him:** Every kingmaker is accustomed to be right and it is not advisable to tell him that he is wrong. You may point out a few important reasons against his proposal, but ask these as questions and don't put these as your comments. Even when he is proved wrong, don't say "I told you so". On the other hand, he may forget the proposal was his and may tell you "how your proposal failed". Don't say "it was yours and not my proposal". Take the blame for the error and you will find him ready to forgive you.

3. **Do what he wants**: You may be tempted to undertake projects that you think will do well for the organisations. Forget that. Do what he thinks is important. The larger the organisation, the less clear are the cause and effect relationships and what the kingmaker says will be accepted. To increase sales, you feel improved advertising is more essential. You work with him on improving advertsiing and let somebody else work on improving distribution channels. If the sales go up, the kingmaker will pronounce that this is due to improved advertising and will reflect some credit on you.

4. **Do it the way he wants:** If he wants to use five colours in a chart, don't show how you can do it with three. If he wants to use 'although', don't use 'though'. Do the job exactly the way he wants.

5. **Talk what he wants to talk about**: The time the kingmaker gives you can be an indication of how close you are to him. Many believe that if the kingmakers are busy, you should stricitly talk business with them and get out quickly when you are finished. This is no

way to stay close to the kingmaker. In fact, you may find him quite free with his time if you talk about things that interest him. He may have no time to discuss distribution channels, but he may have all the time to discuss golf or the next office party. To do this, you may have to bend your interests to coincide with his.

6. **Tell him what goes on around:** You are also a channel of communication to him and an important one if you are the first with the news.

7. **Find opportunities for 'personal service':** This need not be as crude as carrying his brief-case for him. But you can always pass on to him the rice you brought from Delhi because you and your wife don't eat rice (This need not be true). You can help him to win his association's election or to draft his talks.

8. **Ask his advice:** Advice is a commodity everybody gives and nobody takes. Yet, it is very important to ask his advice because:

(a) It flatters his ego.

(b) It keeps you in the eyes of his mind i.e. you are kept visible all the time—in case an opportunity pops up.

(c) It may lead him to commit himself regarding your prospects. .

## HOW TO DEAL WITH SUBORDINATES

There are three main groups of people who talk about you. Your boss and/or kingmaker talk about you in a limited circle and the steps you have considered so far may ensure that this talk is not adverse to your reputation. By respecting your competition you may keep your colleagues reasonably non-critical. But unless you take adequate steps, you may have trouble from your subordinates because they know you best; they can talk to a larger circle and people are likely to believe them. In fact they make or mar your reputation. By and large, you will inherit subordinates. Classify them as follows:

1. **Comeptitive:** These chaps are competing actively to get ahead. Keep them in competition. Use 'handicapping' when necessary to see that the race is kept 'open' till you want to close it.

2. **Submissive:** These chaps have lost their ambition somewhere along the line and would like to continue keeping their job. Security is their greatest need. So pat them on their backs occasionally to reassure them and they will be all right.

3. **Troublesome:** These chaps are a source of nuisance. They may consist of:

(a) **The Frustrated:** Including the chap who was aspiring for your job and did not get it.

(b) **The Politician:** Who has been keeping his job just by playing politics.

(c) **The Incompetent:** Who made 'mistakes' and should never have been there.

There are two temptations that you must avoid when dealing with the 'torublesome'. The first is the missionary urge to reform them. Most of the time this game is not worth the candle. The second is a direct attack declaring these people unwanted. No organisation likes to accept its mistakes openly and your declaring a number of them would put you against the organisation. This you cannot win.

So the effective way to get rid of them is to declare these people valuable but in dire need of proper 'placement'. If they are in a line job, recommend a staff job to take full advantage of their creativity, analytical ability and imagination (displayed in creating rumours and spreading gossip). If they are in a staff job, recommend a line job to use their "initative, aggressiveness and leadership"

84

(displayed in starting and organising trouble in the department). If the organisation is big enough, there is sufficient lack of common knowledge and this will help you to get rid of the 'troublesome'. Do not mind if they get promoted in this process. In big organisations, 'passengers' can be carried at all levels.

## HOW TO DEAL WITH 'OTHERS'

You have been correct with your boss and/or your kingmaker. You are o.K. with your colleagues and subordinates. Does that mean you do not bother about 'others'?

Many a man is walking in the streets of Calcutta (or Bombay or Delhi or Madras) because he made the mistake of neglecting and antagonising 'others'. It may not be obvious as to how the receptionist, the telephone operator, the secretary of the boss or the old-timer brooding in the corner can help you. In fact, they may not be able to help you, yet they can cause trouble at opportune moments if they don't like you.

So keep everybody on your right side. Go out of your way to put in a kind word or a smile. It may reap fabulous returns.

## HOW TO AVOID A 'FALL'

Use of defensive management techniques will enable you to rise high. However, the higher the rise, the bigger can be the fall. To avoid such a fall, it is necessary to observe the following Safety Rules for Defensive Managers:

1.  **Don't identify yourself with any decision**: This means:

    (a) Avoid the necessity of making a decision if you can.

    (b) If you cannot avoid, try to make it a committee decision to spread the responsibility.

85

(c) Particularly where decisions are likely to be unpopular, keep out of them (even out of the committees) by going on tour or on training or falling sick at the appropriate time.

2. **Accept responsibility, but not accountability**: Accept jobs, but don't accpet any target dates. Don't commit on the quality or quantity of output. This will enable you to delegate the job by virtually abdicating it to somebody.

3. **Don't stretch your neck out:** Encourage others to do so. The pyramid at the top tends to be narrow and a few chopped heads can create some comfortable space.

4. **Keep a high degree of activity:** The distinction between work and useful work is difficult—even for experts. For most people (above and below) a high rate of activity signifies a high level of efficiency. So keep everybody busy duplicating or triplicating a job if required.

5. **Keep cribbing about lack of staff and other facilities—in quality and in quantity**: This helps you to:

   (a) Keep the staff you have as your complaints discourage people to have a close look at your current over-staffing.

   (b) Give a ready excuse in case of failures.

## HOW TO DEFEND AGAINST AN ECONOMY DRIVE

In every organisation, sometime or the other, there will·be a drive for economy. Some people believe this is due to recession, otherwise adverse economic conditions, expansion of the company, contraction of the company, etc. However, studies have indicated that the economy drives are more related to the sun-spots than any earthly phenomena.

A Defensive Manager will avoid the tempation of fighting the economy drive. He will lie low till the drive is over and the sunspots return to normal.

Where the Defensive Manager has to show some activity, he should consider the following defensive techniques against the economy drive:

1. **Declare Full Co-operation:** Declare your wholehearted support to the economy drive. Very often this by itself satisfies the Power and eliminates the need for further action.

2. **Declare Some Staff Surplus:** Where more active participation is expected, you can do that by delcaring part of your 'troublesome' staff surplus. Probably nobody would have them so this would not matter. It is better if you can palm off some of them—then you have vacancies you can fill up when the tide of economy is over.

'C' items you should consider are: Stationery pads (use) of blank side of used paper for rough work), erasers (put up a slogan 'Scratch, don't erase'), taxi fare (Compel travelling by bus and tram), etc.


### WHERE DOES THIS LEAD YOU

Defensive management will lead you very high. It will do wonders for you in terms of status and the emoluments and perquisites that go with the status. The higher up you go, the lesser will be your contribution. However, it will be noticed less and less and your reputation for getting along will spread.

What it will do to the organisation is, of course, a secondary matter. Many others may follow your example and your organisation might be full of flashy, smart "yes" men. This might be catastrophic for the organisation and its future. But then, you might retire long before that!

# managerial public
# speaking

NOT too long ago, we used to associate lecturing with social, political or religious leaders. The social leaders used to tell us how social reforms like educating women would bring happiness in our home life. The political leaders assured us that the panacea of all our ills is political freedom and once we become independent, we would have nothing to worry about. The religious leaders talked about assorted ways of reaching Nirvana.

We now have educated women all around including some at home. However, I wonder whether the happiness at home has increased substantially. After independence, we seem to have more problems than ever before. As for Nirvana, more religious leaders seem to be preaching unending varieties, but attainment is still rather rare.

During those days, managers were rather a quiet lot. Most people believed that managers, like children, should be seen not heard.

But things have changed. Today, managers have burst into public speaking en-masse. Starting with Chairmen and Managing Directors, the disease has caught in. Formerly, a typical shareholders' meeting was attended by about a dozen persons who found nothing better to do and the only questions raised were about either the dividend declared or the possibility of a bonus issue. The Chairman's speech used to be a small one, limited to comparing this year's operations with last year's operations, patting the government if they had not. Today the audience remains about covering many a field under the sun. They not only contain comments about social, economic and political situations, but also cover such complex matters as 'Motivation', 'Operations research', 'Leadership', 'Management ethics',' 'Communication,' etc. Obviously, while the talk is actually delivered to a dozing dozen of shareholders, it is really intended for a much wider circulation through printed handouts.

Imitation of the top has been long recognised as the sure way to success in industrial organisations, Consequently, it is not surprising that the middle and lower managers have taken a cue from the top and have started on a talking spree. Any manager worth his designation today is good enough for talking on at least half a dozen subjects. This does not necessarily mean that he has to have six or more separate talks. It is generally enough to have a few separate introductions and conclusions. If proper connections are fabricated the body of the talk can remain the same.

There have been various public speaking courses which are aimed at turning managers into accomplished public speakers. Whilst these courses emphasize the style, not enough useful instruction is available on the contents. In fact, most of the public speaking courses assume that the speeches are given because the managers have something to say. When one has something to say, it is not very difficult to talk. The real difficulty lies in talking when one has nothing to say. When hundreds of managers are talking, all of them would not have much to say. By and large, talks of managers are arranged on the basis of their designations. Getting a designation, however, rarely depends upon the original thinking ability of the individual. One can become a manager through several ways and most of them do not involve the possibility that one would have to say something original.

It is interesting to all and instructive to the newcomers in the managerial field to learn the way of managerial public speaking i.e. to learn "how to talk without really talking".

## CHOOSING A SUBJECT

A manager who is going to talk without really talking, need not worry much about the title of his talk. As noted earlier, it is possible to give the same talk under various titles. However, it is preferable to have a very general title which should be high-sounding with broad implications. For example, "Problems of Management Development" is a better topic to talk nothing about rather than "Use of Bulletin Board for Communication with the Workers"

Thus managers should choose very broad subjects, e.g.:

1. Role of Manager

2. Manager and Motivation

3. Communication and Manager

4. Management and Leadership

5. Decision-making and Management

Even a non-expert will easily note that the same talk can be given under any of these titles.

## STARTING THE TALK

This is the most difficult part of the job, because this involves fitting the ready-made body to the title of the speech. The three main methods available are:

1. Definitive Method

2. Canned-humour Method

3. Autobiographical Method

**Definitive Method:** In this method, each word of the title is defined using as many dictionaries as possible. The objective of using many dictionaries is to create enough confusion to make the audience forget the title of the speech. Then the manager is free to proceed with the body of his talk before the audience can recover. For example:

"Today, we are talking on the vital subject "Communication and Management". Communication, according to Chamber's Twentieth Century Dictionary, is: "giving a share of, imparting, revealing, bestowing, having something in common with another, partaking of Holy Communion, correspondence, connecting passes or channel," Webster defines communication as...." "Management is define as "the act of commanding or controlling or bringing round to one's plans or conducting with great carefulness or training by exercise (as a horse), skilful treatment or administration..."

This reveal the fact that "communication is management and management is communication..." (now the main body can be fitted to this introduction.

**Canned-humour Method:** This again involves use of reference books. However, instead of dictionaries, one uses books of anecdotes. Old copies of Readers Digest may help—but the anecdote books are now classified and it is easier to select a joke somewhat connected to the title of the talk. The technique is to arouse sufficient laughter at the introduction so that when you start on the main body of your talk, the opening sentences are lost in the laughter and the audience cannot catch that the main body has nothing to do with the title. (Since one cannot always be sure that the people will laugh sufficiently loud at one's jokes, it is wise to get half a dozen friends with a loud laugh to attend the talk). The following is an example of such a start.

"When I think of motivation, I remember the famous Mexican story of Pedro. Pedro is a village idiot and, like all idiots, has an ever-watchful neighbour. On a weekly marketing day, the neighbour sees Pedro going down the road to the market in the morning with something concealed in his hands.

94

"What have you got in your hands, Pedro?" asks the neighbour.

"I have got a butterfly," replies Pedro.

"What are you doing with a butterfly, Pedro?" asks the neighborur.

"I shall exchange the butterfly for a pound of butter," replies Pedro.

"You can't do that, Pedro!" says the neighbour.

"Wait and see", says Pedro.

That evening, the neighbour sees Pedro returning with a packet of butter!

Next weekly marketing day, the neighbour again sees Pedro going down the road to the market in the morning with something concealed in the hands.

"What have you got in your hands, Pedro?" asks the neighbour.

"I have got a horsefly," replies Pedro.

"What are you doing with a horsefly, Pedro?" asks the neighborur.

"I shall exchange the horsefly for a horse," replies Pedro.

"You can't do that, Pedro!" says the neighbour.

"Wait and see", says Pedro.

That evening, the neighbour sees Pedro returning— leading a horse!

Next weekly marketing day, the neighbour again sees Pedro going down the road to the market in the morning with something concealed in the hands.

"What have you got in your hands, Pedro?" asks the neighbour.

"I have got a lady's finger," replies Pedro.

"Just a minute," says the neighbour, "let me pick up a few from my garden and join you!"

(While the laughter is on)"... This reveals the importance of motivation. In fact, motivation is management and management is motivation..."

**Autobiographical Method:** This consists of personal remembrances relating to some well-known person—preferably dead. Thus, when you are talking on management and communication, you may mention the time you met Jawaharlal Nehru at Palam Airport and how he agreed that leadership is vital and how he listened to your ideas on the subject. By implication you suggest to the audience that Nehru's untimely death soon after the talk deprived the country of the benefits of the implementation of your suggestions. While the audience is awed at this thought, you can slip into the main body of your speech.

## THE MAIN BODY OF THE TALK

This may require compilation from several books involving a lot of work. However, once a good main body is assembled it can last a manager for years. If the manager is a very frequent lecturer, he many review the talk every three months. Otherwise, an annual revision is adequate.

There are two main poses one may take in preparing the main body of the speech:

1. Speaking-as-an-expert Pose
2. Speaking-as-a-layman Pose

**Speaking-as-an-expert Pose:** This pose is most convenient when you are talking to an assorted group. It is somewhat risky to talk as an expert to the experts—although this is known to have been done. For example, the usual ignoramus manager may find it difficult to talk on "Operations Research" to a seminar of operations research specialists—unless he is talking immediately after a heavy lunch. The real target of an 'expert' talk is the non-expert audience. An accomplished speaker should give two specific impressions in his 'expert' talk. Firstly, that he is bending down to make the subject intelligible at the level of the audience. Secondly, the expertise he is displaying is just the visible part of the iceberg—much more lies in the depth. .

To prepare an "expert" speech, one may follow any of the three main approaches:

(a) Mathematical Approach

(b) Behavioural Science Approach.

(c) Spiritual Approach

**Mathematical Approach:** According to this approach, you scatter your talk with mathematical terminology. For example, you may say: "Management is a function of communication and a derivative of human relations. It is the first integral of leadership and is the square root of economic success", By and large, the audience you get consists of persons who have left their mathematics years ago. Even when they had it, most of them had a rather antagonistic relationship with it. Consequently, the terminology proves quite impressive though it makes no sense.

**Behavioural Science Approach:** This is becoming increasingly fashionable since behavioural science is the rage of modern management. In a behavioural science-based talk, one has to use the appropriate jargon. For example, you may say such things as "communication is the fourth dimension of management; it signifies the efficacy of interaction between groups with repsect to their aspiration and goals modified by environments". It is very important to check the spellings of the various terms involved as even the most accomplished typists are likely to commit errors is typing behavioural science jargon.

**Spiritual Approach:** For the lazy manager who does not want to thumb through the mathematical terminology or the behavioural science jargon, the best way to prepare a speech is to use the spiritual approach. In this approach, you start with 'our culture and tradition'. Thus, talking about communications, you may say that the world got started due to communcation between Eve and the Serpent. If you want to stick to Hindu culture, you may talk about the Vedas and Upanishads and how man communicated with nature thousands of years ago. You may also mention that television was available in the days of Mahabharata and airborne communication was available in the times of Ramayana. (Our audiences like to feel that even if they are technically backward today, their ancestors ages ago were far advanced.) You may then give a sudden spiritual turn saying that real communication "is that between the 'self' and the 'selfless". "What are all communications worth," you may exclaim, "if thou dost not communicate with me?" We Indians are particularly fond of listening to infinite words covering indefinite ideas.

**Speaking-as-a-layman Pose:** This is particularly convenient in talking to a gathering of experts. Here one does not really talk. One poses problems for the experts and asks them to work towards solutions for the lasting benefit of India (or the world—in the case of international gatherings). It is quite in order to suggest all kinds of hare-brained solutions without any responsibility—an advantage of the layman pose. It is also in order to describe how you solved some typical problems through common-sense—without the technical expertise of industrial engineering or operations research or data processing. This emphasises the dispensability of such experts and keeps them in their place (which is subordinate to that of the managers).

**THE CONCLUSION**

Here again, like the introduction, the main problem is to connect the main body of the talk to its title. Where the talk has been soporfic, the conclusion is immaterial as most of the audience wakes at the sound of sudden silence at the end of the talk. Where the audience has been kept awake due to other disturbances, one may use a lengthy anecdote—which due to its length and humour may get the audience to forget the main body of the talk and allow one to slip in:

"To sum up, I may state again that decision-making is the most vital part of management. It is so vital that one may well say that decision-making is management and management is decision-making."

An alternate method is to use a quotation. Many-a-time, the whole talk is made up of quotations collected from various books. But it is important not to acknowledge this as for unknown reasons, the audience expects a manager to give entirely original ideas. (A professor, on the other hand, is expected to quote from books and this is considered a tribute to his scholarship.) However, a manager is allowed to use a quotation as a conclusion. For obvious reasons, the quotation should be a long one. It is always impressive to use a quotation from a company executive, preferably a foreigner (American is the most impressive, since U.S.A. is the peak of all commercial wisdom).

## ANSWERING QUESTIONS

In the good old days, one could get up, stretch and walk out as soon as the lecture was finished. Now, you can't do that. The lecture is inevitably followed by a question-answer session. There are three main types of persons asking questions. The speaker does not have to really answer the questions—he only has to answer the persons asking the questions. As such, it is important to know their types:

1. **The Green Ones:** These consist of the budding 'junior executives'—mostly fresh out of management institutes. They sincerely believe that they can learn

from the managers. So they come with their notebooks, take copious notes and try to ask for clarifications. The way to deal with this category is to pat them on the back for asking a 'good question'. Rephrase the question and pose it as an answer—giving an impression that the subject is too deep to go further into with novices.

2. **The Grey Ones:** These consist of other experienced managers who want to show the particular audience that they know more about the subjec than the main speaker. They do not really ask questions. They make long statements giving their experiences, which terminate in phrases like "how do you tie this up with what you said..." There is a temptation to ask him to repeat (as you have got lost somewhere half-way in his statement) and/or to state that you did not say what he says you said. A wise speaker gets over this temptation and tackles the situation in either of the following two ways:

(a) **Tit-for-tat Approach:** Make an equally long statement misquoting what 'he said' and thus confuse the whole issue.

(b) **Discretion-a-better-part-of-valour Approach:** Compliment the questioner for an excellent exposition of the subject. Assure him that 'many authorities in the field have the same opinion as his' and then tell him that what you had said was really the complementary aspect and not the contradiction of what he said. This generally makes everybody happy.

3. **The white Ones:** These are the pure academicians who have wandered into the managerial meetings. They are confused by the strange mixture of various schools of thought and are compelled to ask such question as:

"How do you reconcile the autocratic leadership pattern with Theory Y of McGregor?"

100

"How does your earlier exposition of motivation tie up with your later illustration of managerial grid?"

The only way for managers to deal with professors is to snub them. Do not get drawn into theoretical arguments. Make such irrelevant statements as, "this, my young man, is practice—and not theory," or "this is the practical application of McGregor (or managerial grid) under Indian conditions".

## CHAIRING A TALK

The ordeal of the talk is not over, even with the end of the question-and-answer-session. The last item to endure is the Chairman's talk. There are two main types of Chairmen:

1. **The Non-listening Chairman:** This is a semi-professional person with an infinite ability to stay awake without listening. When the time comes to close, he gets up and mutters the familiar "thanks-for-the-interesting-and-enlightening-exposition - which - leaves - nothing - to - be added"

2. **The Listening Chairman:** This is a frustrated speaker who takes the opportunity of the closing remarks to make his own speech. He generally takes indifferent notes when the main speaker is talking and uses them to misquote. This type of chariman should be avoided at all costs, since he not only further confuses the audience, but also detains them for intolerable minutes at a time when their patience is at a low ebb.

## WHAT IS WRONG WITH ALL THIS?

Normally, one may write off managerial public speaking as a harmless pastime—something on par with their golf. However, the following aspects make this pastime rather alarming:

101

1. Managerial public speaking is increasingly substituting serious thinking: The managers are so busy sprouting around that they find very little time to think seriously about their own role.

2. Speaking is often considered an adequate substitute for action: Many managers talk about operations research, market research, human relations, etc. so often in their speeches that they are pscyhologically satiated and do not feel the need for action along the lines of their talk in their own jobs.

# ELEVEN

# trials and tribulations
## of indian executives

## MANAGING FROM THE TOP

AN interesting feature of our industrial concerns today is that very few people play the real management role. It has been truly said that in India management exists only at the top. In many instances, there is nothing like number one, number two, and so on in managerial hierarchy. Management seems to comprise a number one and a lot of number tens. All the major decisions and most of the minor ones have to emanate from the very top. The idea of a number of managers at different levels giving decisions and running operations according to a corporate policy and corporate objectives is still a dream talked about mainly in management seminars. In actual life, the managers tend to be 'implementers' whose task is to implement the decisions given by the top management. The spirit of "their's not to reason why" prevails in most organisations. Very often, when the managers are questioned as to why a particular decision has been taken, they point to the top management the same way as the farmer points to the sky when his son inquires why they are having floods. In fact, the word 'policy decision' has become synonymous with an incomprehensible mode of operation.

In this type of atmosphere, the executives find it difficult to exert themselves as 'managers'. Their role continues to be that of the agent in the feudal economy whose job was to get work done by the ryot for the zamindars. In the feudal days, very often it was this agent who was hated more than the zamindar and therefore it is not surprising that in the recent labour unrest, the creatives were the ones who were gheraoed and harassed rather than the owners and proprietors. To this basic difficulty, our executives have .contributed substantially in the following ways to make their role ineffective:

1. Lack of professionalism in their function

2. Lack of insight in other functional areas

3. Lack of integrated approach to management problems

4. Tendency towards obsolescence

5. Lack of macro concept

6. Lack of social conscience

## PULLING EACH OTHER DOWN

The Indian executives have failed to develop professionalism in their basic function. This does not mean that they do not belong to professional associations or institues. In fact, if anything, they belong to too many institute which very often exist mostly on letterheads. Consequently, such institutes are rarely used to develop norms of professional competence, provide facilities for increasing the competence and to establish a code of ethical conduct. It is, therfore, not surprising that the executives have failed to establish any basis of reputation; we can hardly name a successful executive who is acclaimed by fellow professionals. In general, the executives tend to pull each other down by showing cynicism whenever the achievements of any particular one are being talked about. This pulling down of each other has oviously resulted in the entire group being pulled down. I may mention just one indication of this situation. While cinema actors, atheltes, singers, doctors, etc. have been recognised by national awards like Padma Vibhushan, we cannot name a single executive who has qualified for even a Padma Shree. Parkinson has mentioned that the acid test of professionalism is the pride fellow-professionaals take when the highest amongst them is honoured and the concern they feel when the lowest paupered. The executives in India have failed in both aspects of this test.

Our executive flourished well—in spite of his functional deficiency—in the scarcity economy, when no superior professional skills were demanded. The situation is changing fast and functional excellence will be a must in the near future.

## THE GREAT IGNORAMUS

The next problem with our executive is his complete ignorance of the other functional areas of management. The running war between production and sales is well known. Their antipathy to the accountants comes only a close second to that towards each other. Typically, sales executives take an attitude that the lack of co-operation from the production executives and the constant nagging from the accountants are the only obstacles that prevent them from reaching high altitudes of achievement. Left to themselves, they would probably sell innumerable varieties at any price. Rarely you meet a sales executive who has a clear insight into the production problems and the cost-structure of his products.

Similarly, most of the production executives are constantly complaining about the changes in production programmes. From their talk it would seem that the organisation is intended to produce goods which can give maximum technical efficiency—with no relevance to the market. Frequently, a weaving master goes into mourning on the withdrawal of a particular sort of weave because it used to give him a better production efficiency. Similarly, spinning masters crave for better cotton mixings to improve their production efficiency. In fact, the production executives rarely worry about the market situation or the profitability of their products. I have rarely found a weaving master who could say which part of the country his cloth is destined for or at what profit he expects the cloth to be sold. When the controls were introduced and prices were stamped on the product, that was the first time that many production executives became aware of the selling prices.

This attitude of insulation has cause considerable difficulties in many areas. In foundries, production executives have aided and abetted workers to produce big size casting which were not in demand—even when smaller castings were in demand and had to be obtained from outside. The big size castings increased the production in terms of tonnage and also increased the wages of the workers which were tied up with the tonnage. This led to a queer phenomenon:

The concern was having a high inventory of castings of big size while they were actually purchasing from outside smaller castings.

The non-finance executives have been very naive also regarding the finance and accounting area. The executives are happy to remain insulated from the basic accounting relevant to their job. They are happy to state that they don't understand accounting—leaving the accounting decision to the accountant—and only moan their loss of production efficiency or sales.


## WANTED: AN INTEGRATED APPROACH

The ignorance about other functional areas characteristic of most managers has divided the organisation into so many insulated comparments, that coordinated and fully informed decisions are a rare phenomena. In developed countries a large number of people representing many professional disciplines get together to exchange ideas and to formulate industrial decisions regarding innovation and production. In India, the initiative for change has to come from the top.

In the developed economy, the scientist, the finance man, the marketing man and the production man all play an active part in making things happen. The scientist is considered a valuable consultant to industry as he is essential for innovation. The financial man familiarises himself with modern techniques of production and marketing so as to give new business ideas. The financial experts thus use their knowledge to encourage new lines and business activities. The marketing man probes customers for fundamental attitudes towards company products, determines sales strategies and analyses product design and pricing. All these people form a part of a team with the production man. Marketing is understood as an integral system from product conception to product consumption. Unless this type of integrated concept is developed, we shall continue to have insulated compartments which spend most of their efforts and creative abilities in countering each other—rather than helping each other towards common objectives. This remindes me of an incident. I found that one of my hostelmates in the United States was from the navy of an Asian country. He seemed to have a very high sounding rank so I asked him about the size of their navy When he described it, I was rather surprised to find that they were keeping a big navy. "Why do you have such a big navy when you haven't fought a war for the last few hundred years?" I asked. He replied, "What do you mean by we have not fought a war? In our country our navy fights our army". It is not surprising, therefore, that they have a strong army too. In many of our organisations various departments strengthen themselves mainly to counter the strength of other departments. The development with this attitude is of no help to the organisational objectives.

Another important aspect in which the insulation plays a damaging role is the attitude of executives to labour. Many production executives tend to believe that the personnel function belongs to the personal or labour officer who is always around to face the problem. Unless it is realised that personnel is not an isolated function—but is an integral part of every executive's function, it is difficult to get any effective personnel policy in operation. There is a tendency for the personnel managers to take line decisions and dominate over the other executive who have not studied any aspect of personnel problems.

## HANGING SWORD OF OBSOLESCENCE

The next problem about our executives is their lack of aptitude for continuous learning. It has been well remarked that half of our knowledge becomes obsolete in ten years. Unless continual reinforcement is available the executives can easily become obsolete. The executives in India are the most educated illiterates that can be found anywhere in the world. Most of them barely read their daily newspaper— and that is often the beginning and the end of their reading activity. They always complain about lack of time. However, lack of time, if correctly translated, means lack of priority Reading or acquiring new knowledge and insights gets a very low priority in the case of our executives. Business lunches, cocktail parties and weekened golf leaves very little time for any meaningful knowledge-acquiring activity. Time and again, in the management seminars of the residential type, executives have confessed that they have read in a few weeks of the seminar more than what they did in twenty years of their industrial career from the day they joined their first job.

It is difficult to see how the executives can keep up with the times if they do not study the impcat of technological innovations, socio-economic and political changes and the new mangement techniques on the aspirations, needs and expectations of the consuming public. Executives have to make an active effort on their own to gather this new knowledge and to get an insight in the way they have to change their strategies to suit the changing environment. Just as we cannot afford to "spend" all the money we get,

110

we have to "invest" some of it in insurance, shares etc., We cannot afford to 'spend' all our time on current operations. We must 'invest' some of it to protect ourselves from becoming obsolete. In fact, when improved machinery is available, salesmen will form a queue to demonstrate to the executives the merits of the new fruits of technology Newly developed techniques in the field of quantitative methods or in the area of behavioural sciences have no salesmen peddling their goods. Executives have to make efforts on their own to gather these new ideas and to get an insight in what way these ideas can be of relevance to their environement.

## "PEACE IN OUR TIMES"

Sometime this opposition to new ideas is due to the approach of "peace in our times" by executives who have only a few years to go. They would rather continue doing a job they were accustomed to rather than change to a new method involving new problems. Some suspect that the difficulties in our public sector are basically due to this situation regarding the top personnel who were civil servants, put on a few years of tenure after their superannuation. It is quite interesting that bright young men trained in modern management techniques are made to work in obscure corners with a minimum of responsibility while tottering old men who are already obsolete are asked to run corporations which involve investments amounting to hundreds of crores.

Even where the techniques and ideas are forced through management development programmes, there is a tendency to brand them "irrielevant to our conditions". Ways and means are found to get out of the need to make changes. In fact, executives have become the biggest impediment to innovations in our industry. For example, resistance to computers is much greater at the junior and middle management level and at least one computer centre was effectively torpedoed by the antagonism of these executives.

111

A lot of agitation at the staff and worker level against automation is at least encouraged, if not instigated, at the lower and middle level of management.

## INABILITY TO GRASP THE BIG PICTURE

The typical executive is unable to look beyond his own nose--his unit. He cannot grasp in totality the emerging economic picture. This is obvious from his attitude to the public sector industry. While the public sector is growing to increasing dominance, the status of various functional areas in the public sector is inadequate and this has not worried the private sector executives. For example, take the marketing function. To the civil service officials who took charge of the public sector units in the initial stage, marketing activity was a waste of time. They were convinced that products could be sold by issuing a circular. This civil service attitude still persists and very few public sector companies have really effecting marketing operations. There are many companies in the public sector which cannot sell their products even at prices lower than those of their competitiors in the private sector. This is basically because of lack of commitment to delivery schedule, lack of service, lack of flexibility regarding financial arragements, etc. In fact, the public sector flourishes most when they can distribute their products on a "rationing" basis. Wherever they have to do a real marketing job they are in trouble. The public sector is no longer a laughing matter. It has come to stay and it will have an increasing impact on our economy. As such, it is most essential that the public sector operations are put on a commercial basis by strengthening the functional areas. And a great deal of agitation from the private sector executives will be required to achieve this.

# THE INSULTATED EXECUTIVE

The last, but not the least, problem of the executive is his deficiency in the social conscience. The general tendency among executives is to meet and convince each other as to how the current situation is extremely sad and how the labour, the government, the politician—in fact everybody else but the executive is responsible for the mess we are in. The executive is not ready to accpet that there are hardly "we" and "they" in this, in the wonderland of Indian Managers situation. The executive as a part of the society has contributed his bit to the mess. He has managed to insulate himself from the public-at-large. He has given no thought to the needs and the aspirations of the common man and it is no wonder that he has lost the confidence of the common man. The political power is, therefore, moving away from him. Unless he modifies his strategy, he will have even less influence on the major decisions of our environment.

The executives have withdrawn themseelves so much that the government is left to the politicans, statisticians and economists and truly they have ruined the country. Since independence, our academically brightest students looked forward to a career in industry. The first-rate talent thus became the executive. The second-raters became economists and statisticians and the third and fourth-raters went into politics. Yet today, the politicians are ruling and the executives are reduced to simple implementers with no initiative and no ability to control the stream of events. Unless our executives can get out of this rut, there would be no end to their trials and tribulations.

# organising
# for o & m

ORGANISING O & M Groups in companies has been a relatively recent but fast-spreading pastime. In advertisements for management postition, O & M runs well with other current favourites, like management accountants, industrial engineers and data processing personnel. In view of the importance of this activity, a survey was carried out and its brief outline is given in this article concealing the actual identities for obvious reasons.

## WHY HAVE O & M

The management reasoning for having O & M was found to fall in the following four categories which are illustrated by actual experts from the survey:

### 1. Keeping Up with Jones & Co.

...By the way, Bill, I met Harold Jones of Jones & Co. at cocktails yesterday. He was yapping a lot about his new O & M Group. And it seems most of those around are either having something like that or planning to have it. I also told them that we are in the process of organising our O & M. After all, we are almost as big as Jones & Co. and bigger than many others around. So will you get going on this? It seems that not having O & M is almost as bad as not having a golf team in Merchants Cup. And while you are at it, find out what the hell O & M stands for...

### 2. They Have it Back Home

...Here is the latest questionnaire from Home Office. It

(*O&M is abbreviation of Organisation & Methods)

117

seems they are carrying out another survey of the overseas subsidiaries. We can fill up all other blank spaces and tick here and there—but on this one I'm stumped: "What is the strength of your O & M Group and what activities do they cover". Let's get this O & M Group as I don't want them to feel we are not progressive enough. But before you go too far, drop a personal note to Harry Smith of Home Office to find out what the hell O & M means and what they are supposed to do...

### 3. We are in a Mess and it's Getting Worse

... We can't handle this on ad hoc basis any more. The chaps sent on temporary assignments do not seem to be fully effective and in their absence, another mess is created in their jobs. We must get a group which can handle such jobs and organise them properly. Call it O & M or S & P or whatever other letters of the alphabet you like, but get cracking on it quickly...

### 4. Let's Plan Our Functional Organisation

...Now we are O.K. on these production, sales, materials, personnel, finance and secretarial functions. What about the systems function? By that I mean the organisation and processing of information for all our activities. Forms, procedures, office equipment, staffing and organisational studies, data processing and so on. Let's get coordinated O & M and Data Processing Groups...

### HOW TO START O & M

The following excerpts from the survey show similar variations in the management approach to the installation of the O & M Groups:

### 1. Rose by any name

...Yah, we've got to get his O & M started quickly. Now what is that Raman doing? ...Oh, looking after the canteen and the company magazine? I'm sure that cannot take all his time. Anyway we can give him an assistant if necessary. Call him O & M Manager from the next 1st and ask all departments to send him any forms or procedures they require advice on. I don't think many will bother...

## 2. Now We Can Shunt him By

...We want to promote Krishnan on this sales post but Basu might be a problem there... Yes, why not have a little shunting around, let Basu be the Head of O & M, so we won't have to worry about him for sometime. I guess sooner or later he will find something to do there. If worst comes to worst, we may send him to training courses and keep him busy...

## 3. Blue-eyed boy

... Let's put Mr. Smart Alec as the Head of O & M. I know he has no experience in anything, but then that will give him a fresh outlook. And put those remaining management trainees that nobody wants in this group so that we can have a young dynamic team...

## 4. Old work-horse: (This is actually a variation of the blue eyed boy approach—using grey hair instead.)

... So, Khanna just cannot handle his department. Well, he has been with us for 20 years, so we can't get him sacked and he has another 20 years to retire. Let's put him up as the Head of O & M and put under him the chaps rendered surplus when we closed the Bhagalpur Depot. Then this O & M business will virtually cost us nothing. The chaps are not doing anything now, so what does it matter if they don't do anything in O & M?...

## 5. Let's Get the Right Type

... Are the job descriptions and job requirements lists ready for all the O & M positions?... Let's circulate them amongst the managers so that they can

119

recommend suitable chaps. Also put advertisements in all leading papers. We shall give aptiude tests and see the candidates from within and outside our organisation and select the most suitable.

## HOW TO OPERATE O & M

The variation noted in the survey are as follows:

### 1. The Spanish Inquisition Approach

...You better·start with the Purchasing Department Half the chaps are supposed to be out in the market, but I'm sure they are just loafing. The others are most of the time talking with visitors—and not all of the visitors are suppliers. So you should be able to cut down the staff by at least 50 per cent. Tell the Purchasing Head that he better agree to that or else...

### 2. Quadruplicate Form Approach

... Those who desire O & M services, should fill in Form No. 420 in quadruplicate giving all the details required and attaching all detailed calculations, drawings, etc. covering the expected resultant advantages. This form should be routed through Departmental Manager—General Manager—Director—Managing Director—Administration Director—General Manager—O·& M Manager to reach the undersigned at least three months before the requested commencement of the assignment...

### 3. Peddle Yourself Approach

... As O & M Man, you must be able to sell—yourself, your services and your recommendations. What is so difficult about convincing the Chief Accountant that he can do with 4 less staff except at the time of annual closing and even then he can manage with 3 less provided there is nobody on casual, sick or privilege leave? ...I know it will make his life difficult, but then that's where the selling comes in...

#### 4. Fire Brigade Approach

...Our auditor tells me that the plant stores is in a terrible mess, will you look into it personally at once.....And the operating report to the Managing Director was delayed this month by a fortnight—just look into that right away so that it is not delayed next month... Another urgent problem is the procedure for agency handling; the sales are waiting for that for over a months and they have started screaming... And...

#### 5. Management by Objectives Approach

...Now that the general divisional objectives for the next year are ready, let each department manager plan his own detailed objectives and get together with O & M to find out in what areas O & M can render useful service.

# dummy haves
## versus
## dummy have-nots

IN India, socialism is more heard of than seen. Recently it has become particularly vociferous and the slogans of 'remove poverty' have drowned all other issues. The impression given is that the war between the haves and have-nots has really started in full earnest.

This is probably the greates hoax of modern times!

What is really taking place is only a fake war between the dummy haves and the dummy have-nots!!

## THE CRAZY PYRAMID

In the traditional analysis, the pyramid of society is divided into the upper class, the middle class and the lower class.

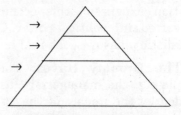

1. Upper class   →
2. Middle class   →
3. Lower class   →

**Traditional Pyramid**

The progressive tax-structure prevalent in most democratic countries (as shown on the next page) has tended to flatten the pyramid and contract the upper class. In a country like England, the upper class has been considerably diminished since the Second World War.

125

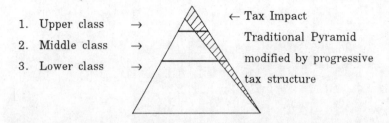

1. Upper class  →
2. Middle class  →
3. Lower class  →

← Tax Impact
Traditional Pyramid
modified by progressive
tax structure

In India, the prevalent tax-structure has created a crazy pyramid consisting of four distinct sections:

1. **The Real Haves:** These are the few people whose large assets and incomes have avoided or evaded the taxes. As a result, there has been a phenomenal growth in their assets and economic power. Since no election can be fought

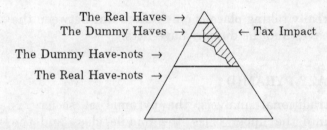

The Real Haves  →
The Dummy Haves  →
The Dummy Have-nots  →
The Real Have-nots  →

← Tax Impact

without black money (in view of the unrealistic limits on election expenses), this economic power is continually converted into political power. Consequently, in spite of all socialistic measures, the real haves are having a field day!

2. **The Dummy Haves:** These are the high-salaried people e.g. the managerial class whose income is greatly eroded by the impact of the 'progressive' taxes they have been submitting to and the high standard of living them are pressured into. They seem to have a high 'revenue' income which vanishes before it can be converted into 'assets'.

3. **The Dummy Have-nots:** These are the employees of the organised sector of our industry. Their income is always represented as grossly inadequate—as they keep comparing it with the income of the dummy haves (before

taxes). Something, they compare their income with those carrying out similar work in the developed countries. This is the class that shouts socialism the loudest.

4. **The Real Have-nots:** Since Independence, we have invested considerable resources in development and these have resulted in some benefits. However, the economy has been short-circuited and the benefits have gone only to the the real haves, the dummy haves and the dummy have-nots—leaving a large majority of our people high and dry. These real have-nots, i.e. the landless labour, farmers with uneconomic land-holdings, workers in unorganised sector of our industry, etc., have not seen any betterment of their lot.

## PENSIONABLE DACOITY

The miserable lot of our real have-nots can be demonstrated statistically in terms of per capita income, etc. However, in our country nobody believes in statistics, unless the statistics support the viewpoint of the person concerned. I feel the following two factual episodes illustrate the situation much more effectively:

1. During the 1971 mid-term Lok Sabha election campaign, the Samyukta Socialist Party put up a dramatic poster "Would you vote for Badri Prasad or for Indira". This character Badri Prasad was a gardner employed by Mrs. Indira Gandhi on a monthly salary of Rs 80/—. The S.S.P. held that Indiraji was 'exploiting" Badri Prasad for such a pittance and thus was not a real socialist. When the political speakers of the Party put forth a rhetoric denouncing this exploitation, they found to their surprise that the rural audience could not see any "exploitation"! In fact, they felt that an income of nearly Rs 1,000 per annum was handsome indeed—and only a small minority amongst them could boast of such an income.

127

2. In order to deal with the dacoity menace in Chambal Valley in a constructive way, the Sarvodaya Movement decided to give Rs 17/— per month each to the families of dacoits killed in action. The idea was to assist the families in bringing up their children in the normal way of life— otherwise they had to dopt dacoity as the only available profession and dacoits were becoming hereditary—as business tycoons in our industry. When a Sarvodaya worker visited some of the villages for a feed-back, she was surprised to find that the rural population felt that the Sarvodaya Movement was encouraging the dacoity profession. So far the only consideration that prevented an adventurous young man to take dacoity as a profession, they felt, was the possible plight of his survivors. With the Sarvodaya people giving pensions, there was nothing to bar these adventurous young men from plunging into dacoity.

## THE EASY WAY

All our great and numerous socialists have done pretty little for these real have-nots. They have concentrated their efforts in organising the dummy have-nots—as it is much easier to do so. There is a story of a man who was searching under a street-light. A friend passing by asked him, "What have you lost?" "My ring", said the man. The friend also joined in the search. After a few minutes the friend asked, "Where exactly have you dropped it?" "Over there", replied the man, pointing at a dark corner a few yards away. "Then why don't you search there?" asked the friend. "Oh, no!" replied the man, "it is much easier to search under the light".

The socialistic efforts through organisation of trade unions have been mainly for the dummy have-nots trying to give them more and more. Thus, sweepers getting Rs 300/- per month are represented as the poor exploited men deserving much more.

## THE TEDDY BEAR APPROACH

In fact, most of the attack the dummy have-nots have mounted is based not on the consideration of what those who are higher up deserve or don't deserve, but on the consideration that they do not get these benefits. There is a story of a man who took his old father to a psychiatrist. "There is something seriously wrong with my father", said the man. "Well, it is rather sad", said the psychiatrist, "however, he seems to be about 80 years old and this seems to be a harmless obsession." "But you don't understand, doctor", said the man, "the teddy-bear belongs to me."

## RETIREMENT ON EIGHT LEGS

While the socialistic slogan of the dummy have-nots is a fake, so is the capitalistic defensive posture of the dummy haves. Every socialistic measure of the government raises a clamorous protest from the dummy haves when they have really nothing much to lose any more. They have a large revenue income which is considerably diminished by the taxes they have to pay. With the remaining income they have to meet the many essential and expensive luxuries that they have unwittingly accustomed themselves to. As a result, they can hardly acquire any assets—in spite of years and years of work. When the prospects of retirement face them, they get into a crisis as they find that with their retirement benefits drastically eroded by inflation, they cannot afford even the rental of a flat in a city like Bombay. With no roots elsewhere, they have to stick to the urban area and have to seek employment to continue living at the standard they have been accustomed to. When no employment is available they become "consultants".

The situation is even more accentuated in the case of government servants and ministers. These are the maharajahs of the modern time—who are ready to resort to any means to keep their source of luxuries. The civil service used the public sector as their 'Panjrapol' where they could continue to enjoy the luxurious life a few years after retirement—and in this process ruined the public sector in its formative years. The humiliations that the politicians undergo to get the election 'ticket' are too blatant to require description. Even ministers are ready to be interviewed 'en masse' to stick to their positions.

This is why it is remarked that nobody in this country retires on two legs. He retires on on eight legs—when four persons carry him to his final rest!

## THE PEOPLE'S CAR SOCIALISM

Due to the peculiar roles played by the dummy haves and the dummy have-nots, we have a fake socialism. The control on car prices is held as a great socialistic measure— although it hardly benefits anybody except a few government officers getting their cars through the government quota. The businessman pays a premium anyway as he cannot wait for years to get the car he needs. The so-called masses walking in the streets need not worry whether the car that may knock one of them costs Rs 20,000 or Rs 25,000! Similar is the situation regarding the "People's Car Project". This is amongst the items which have consumed the maximum government time at the Cabinet level—where time is so scarce. How many amongst the masses can maintain such a car even if it is given free?

These and other such measures reveal that the prevailing attitudes reflect only the dummy socialism tossed amongst the dummy haves and the dummy have-nots.

## WALL-PAPER ON THE CRACKING WALLS

The tragedy of the situation, however, is that this dummy socialism is masking the need for real efforts to improve the lot of the real have nots. The need is becoming increasingly urgent as anti-social groups like the Naxalites are taking advantage of the situation. This is a potentially explosive situation and we cannot waste our time in sticking wall-paper on the cracking walls.

The need of the hour is for the dummy haves and dummy have-nots to come together and plan a campaign to tackle the real haves and to ameliorate the condition of the real have-nots. The need is for a collaboration—and not a fake war—between the dummy haves and the dummy have-nots.

# the last letter of the alphabet of management i.e. theory 'z'

IT all started with late Professor Douglas McGregor's Theories "X" and "Y" representing the traditional 'mukadami' system of management and his new "Involvement" concept of management. This led to the geometrical use of "X" and "Y" coordinates in the managerial Grid by Dr Robert Blake—with the coordinates representing 'Concern for Output' and 'Concern for People'. The gird gave 5 typical management styles as shown in Chart 1 (a) numerical improvement over McGregor's 2 styles.

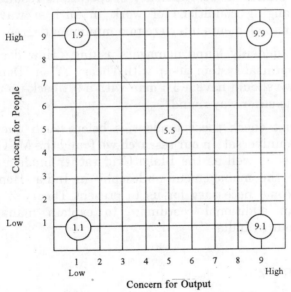

Chart 1—Dr Blake's Management Grid and 5 Typical Management Styles

1.9 Management: Thoughtful attention to the needs of the people for statisfying relationships leads to a comfortable friendly organisation atmosphere and work tempo.

9.9 Management: Work accomplishment is from commited people; inter-dependence through a "common stake" in the organisational purpose leads to relationships of trust and respect.

5.5 Management: Adequate organisational performance is possible through balancing the necessity to get out work with maintaining morale of people at a stisfactory level.

1.1 Management: Exertion of minimum effort to get required work done is appropriate to sustain organisation membership.

9.1 Management: Efficiency in operations results from arranging conditions of work in such a way that human elements interfere to a minimum degree.

So we suddenly found managers asking, "How does this new appraisal system tie-up with Theory Y?" or "Don't you think we should have a 5.5 man with a 9.1 back-up rather than the other way round?"

We must check these tendencies before such questions become universal. In our research we found the Mc-Gregor Theories as well as the Blake Grid rather inadequate to explain the management philosophy in India. Hence, it has become necessary for us to present Theory Z which uses an additional coordinate to explain managerial behaviour in India.

## THEORY 'Z'

The Theory Z is based on the following premises:-

1. An industrial enterprise sooner or later (sooner for private sector, later for public sector) requires some

output to support the workers, clerks and various cadres of managers employed. Thus, some concern for output has to be shown by some managers some time.

2. In order that the employees do not spend all their energies in internal conflicts (e.g. workers vs. supervisors, clerks vs. headclerks, managers vs. managers, managers vs. everybody else) and do spend some effort towards meaningful output. It is necessary to maintain some degree of morale in the organisation. Thus, some concern for people has to be shown by some managers some time.

3. Since everybody is in the game for himself, most of the times most of the people will seek to grind their own axes and show a lot of concern for self.

If we show concern for output on one coordinate, concern for people on another coordinate and concern for self on the third coordinate, we get the 3-D system (shown in Chart II) and the following typical management styles.

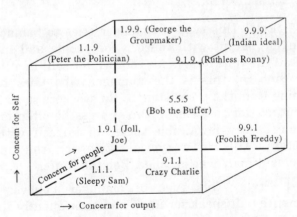

Chart II-Ramasaway-Rangnekar Theory Z
and 9 Typical Management Styles

Chart II Ramaswamy-Rangnekar Theory Z and 9 typical Management Styles

137

1. 1-1-1 Style: Negligible effort to get output maintain morale or promote self. This is typical of a private sector executive who is reaching the retirement age and has been refused an extension, or a public sector executive who is awaiting transfer orders. He is known as the "Sleepy Sam".

2. 9-1-1 Style: Emphasis on output results in arranging conditions of work in such a way that interference of human elements is avoided (e.g. automation)—although this may well result in diminishing the size of the department and affecting adversely the promotion chances of the manager. Such 'Crazy Charlies' are often responsible for whatever output we get out of certain industrial concerns.

3. 1-9-1 Style: This type of manager is reconciled to the fact that he is not going any further and (since he has many years yet to retire) wants to create a friendly atmosphere by maintaining good relations with all around. He naturally avoids nagging anybody for output and hence is known as the "Jolly Joe"

4. 5-5-5 Style: This type of manager tries to balance the concern for output with concern for people and in that effort half the time forgets his concern for self! In a typcial family concern, this is the manager who tries to get something from the proprietors to the workers so as to get some output out of them. In this process he often fails to maintain a very favourable image of himself with the proprietors. This is a typical style for the 'middle management man' who is called 'Bob the Buffer'.

5. 9-9-1 Style: This type of manager believes that performance will speak for itself and consequently spends his entire time on maximising output and morale—and has no time to play company politics and look after himself. When the 'performance speaks' its language is Greek and Latin to the top management interpreters around them translate it to absorb all the credit leaving 'Follish Freddy' high and dry! So Freddy is left to maintain

his performance while others get promoted.

6. 1-1-9 Style: Here is 'Peter the Politician' who spends his entire time playing company politics to promote himself. He cares neither for output nor for other peole—but hopes to get ahead by currying favour with the top management. His existance is parasitic—supported by the Foolish Freddies in the organisation.

7. 1-9-9 Style: This manager believes in 'managing by clique' and creates a group to back him up. This gives rise to other cliques and corresponding loss of attention to output. Such a 'Geoge the Groupmaker' can be quite a menace if he is not controlled in time.

8. 9-1-9 Style: This manager expects to promote himself by giving a high output and bringing it to the attention of the top management. In this process, this 'Ruthless Ronny' treads merrily on various other people and may end up getting blown up if the resentment explodes.

9. 9-9-9 Style: This is the 'Ideal Indian' manager who can get a high level of output from people committed to the organisational objectives—but keeps, all the same, continuous communication with the top management to ensure that he is not robbed of his credit by the company politicians.


**OTHER 3-D STYLES**

Others have evolved 3-D models to illustrate management styles. But these do not represent the characteristics found in the Indian industry. For example, William Reddin has used "Effectiveness" as the third coordinate and has described eight management styles (Chart III next page):

Theory Z, besides giving numerically superior management styles, describes our management styles with greater insight. Jolly Joe is more colourful than his cousin the

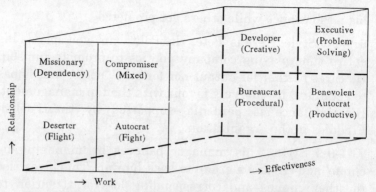

Chart III-Reddin's 3-D Model with 8 Management Styles

Missionary. Similarly, Sleepy Sam is more common in our country than the Deserter. Bob the Buffer is the Indian counterpart of the Compromiser. Ruthless Ronny is more purposeful than either the Simple—or the Benevolent—Autocrat. The Bureaucrats we have are of both the types: Peter the Politican and George the Groupmaker. Developer and Executive types are irrelevant in India—while Reddin's model has failed to reveal Crazy Charlie, Foolish Freddy and the Ideal Indian managers.

This shows how the materialistic dimension (i.e. Effectiveness) fails to give the insight that a philosophical dimension (i.e. Concern for Self) can give for our conditions. This is to be expected, since we are truly a philosophical people deep in the heart of our hearts!

(The author is indebted to Prof. N.S. Ramaswamy for the basic idea.)

140